D1387332

The Politics of Nuclear Disarmament

Militarism, State and Society

Series editor: Dan Smith

Pluto's series on militarism, state and society will provide political analysis as well as new information and argument relating to current political controversies in the field of nuclear weapons, military policy and disarmament. It aims to present radical analyses and critiques of the existing orthodoxies in readable and accessible form.

Martin H. Ryle

The Politics of Nuclear Disarmament

Pluto Press

This edition first published in Great Britain by
Pluto Press Limited, Unit 10, Spencer Court,
7 Chalcot Road, London NW1 8LH

ISBN 0 86104 353 7

Cover drawing by Chris Madden
Cover design by Clive Challis

Typeset by Grassroots Typeset, London NW6 (01-328 0318)
Printed in Great Britain by Mansell Bookbinders
(incorporating Mansell Print) Witham, Essex

Contents

Acknowledgements / 6

Introduction: 'Beyond political choice'? / 7

1. Nuclear Weapons and Civilian Populations / 16

2. Nationalism, Internationalism and
   European Nuclear Disarmament / 33

3. The Case for British Unilateral Nuclear Disarmament / 57

4. Nuclear Weapons and Democracy in Britain / 76

References / 97

Acknowledgements

I should like to thank Dan Smith for his help and advice, both on points of fact (where, of course, I remain responsible for any errors) and in amending and improving my argument in several places.

I should also like to express my indebtedness to Kate Soper, although she knows that no formula exists in which I can begin to do so.

Introduction: 'Beyond political choice'?

From the point of view of the human race, the 'problem' of nuclear weapons admits of only one solution: they must be scrapped. We know that a fraction of the fifty thousand and more warheads now stockpiled would be enough to extinguish civilisation, and there is only one way to make sure that they are never launched.

But although we made thermonuclear weapons, we cower before them, paralysed as before some alien creation. They embody our highest technical ingenuity, and they bespeak the depth of our social barbarism. They witness our mastery over nature, yet their use would place us at the mercy of an unprecedented 'natural' (radiological, climatic, atmospheric, bacteriological, ecological) catastrophe. The materially richest societies of the world devote precious skills and resources to their production, and in doing so undermine their own wealth, jeopardising a precarious economic security for an 'investment' whose only human function is never to be used.

Their abolition, too, seems caught up in paradox. It is 'utopian' and yet minimally necessary for survival, supremely desirable and yet 'impossible'. If we wish our species to have a future, nothing is clearer than the urgency of scrapping the nuclear stockpiles. Meanwhile this goal recedes and recedes, so that few politicians seem to regard it as attainable, and most ordinary people appear — or appeared until recently — to have 'learned to live with the Bomb'. Perhaps insurmountable obstacles prevent our ever attaining this goal which all human reason tells us we must reach, or perish? Dr Lawrence Freedman is certainly not expressing an eccentric view when he concludes that: 'the overbearing role of nuclear weapons in contemporary international affairs is now... virtually beyond political choice'.[1]

But his conclusion must be juxtaposed to the sober judgement of Frank Barnaby: 'to say that nuclear disarmament is impossible in today's world is not only incorrect but may be tantamount to saying that nuclear war is inevitable'.[2] 'Beyond political choice'? — but that, after all, is no statement of fact, it is itself a *political* statement, and politics is, precisely, the contest over what is and what is not open to 'choice'. It is also, and simultaneously, the contest over who makes that choice. 'The role of nuclear weapons' has *got* to be a matter of choice, and it is increasingly plain that it will become so only when effective political power in the 'advanced' nations has been claimed, or reclaimed, from below. For there can be no doubt that 'the peoples of the world' (in the phrase of the World Disarmament Campaign) want nuclear disarmament, and that their political leaders have done less than nothing to secure it.

But to speak of 'the human race', 'the peoples of the world', is to invoke (it will be objected) a state of human consciousness, and of global society, as remote as it is desirable. Meanwhile nuclear weapons cannot be seen, naively, as 'the enemy of the human species': they must be understood as artefacts which people have chosen to build, in a context which cannot be wished away: the double context of human aggression, and of the division of the world into a multitude of sovereign states. One might reply that if aggression, and even acts of homicide, are to be regarded as natural to mankind, we must accord at least equal recognition to our instinct for survival, which today impels us toward disarmament. But in any case modern weapons are not the simple outcome of any human 'propensity'; they exist within a context which is far from biological, and which permits, and demands, social and political intervention. As to the second point, nationalism certainly persists and continues to provoke war; but nuclear weapons nonetheless force us to think of the species and the globe, for it is the species and the globe which they threaten, with unprecedented destruction: it is the context of the embattled nation state, however true to past experience, which today provides an anachronistic and perilously naive framework for the discussion. In this respect nuclear weapons may yet prove to have 'done some good'; they may yet provoke, before it is too late, an essential leap forward in the dialectic between human consciousness and human ingenuity in slaughter, forcing us to order our global society in ways that acknowledge the folly of mutual massacre (a folly always glimpsed even, and especially, in the midst of war itself). The first test of whether they have indeed 'done any good' will of course be whether we can abolish them.

In this sense nuclear disarmament will certainly have to go along with, or immediately precede, a historic change in the nature of international relations. If the world's most powerful states are ever to make war on one another, they will use nuclear weapons — to say nothing of the hideous battery of 'conventional' arms (such as were unleashed by the US military on the people of South-East Asia), and the chemical arsenals currently being developed despite the conventions which outlaw their use. The struggle to abolish nuclear weapons (which today are quite 'legitimately' deployed in terricidal numbers) is the focus of the wider struggle to bring the military under control and to prevent the destructive power of modern technology from being used in future against human beings. We are talking about an end to war — either that, or an end to human civilisation. That is why I do not discuss chemical and biological weapons in this book:[3] if we can scrap the nuclear stockpiles, we shall have won the wider struggle, and we shall have embarked on the road to a peaceful international order, in which the threat of mass murder will no longer be an 'option' in the conduct of foreign policy.

Where I differ from some earlier commentators[4] — and where I believe that today's CND differs from the movement of the sixties — is in rejecting the notion that this change to a more peaceful international community can simply be imposed from above by some unifying 'authority' (perhaps itself armed with the latest implements of genocide). The world's governing elites are wedded to a militarism which is fundamentally at odds with the needed change. And of course this is not just a matter of how our rulers think; it is how they maintain their power. The ruling classes of the 'advanced' nations, East and West, dominate not just the peoples of hostile and less 'advanced' nations, but their own domestic populations, by their monopoly of the means of destruction. If we can disarm the military, we shall not just free our 'enemies' from the threat of

10

annihilation; we shall also free ourselves. For, internationally, we are each other's, and thus our *own* enemies: collectively, we, civilians everywhere, are the potential victims of the military elites which we maintain to threaten each other, and which now operate, within every state, at the very limits of democratic control. The struggle to regain that control must come from below, and must take place across national boundaries. In today's disarmament movement, the twin themes of democracy and internationalism are inextricably linked together.

If it is objected that this is still to argue in abstractions, it is possible to point in reply to one region of the world where such themes are the currency of an emerging political movement. In Europe, after two fratricidal wars in the space of forty years, it is hard to detect enthusiasm for further slaughter. National identity is still jealously guarded, and economic rivalry persists; locally, religious, national and ethnic minorities still resort to arms; but the danger for Europeans is plainly not that these factors will lead to another all-out war, but that our continent, learning to live in peace internally, will be destroyed in a battle between the superpowers who divided it up in 1945 — destroyed, this time, beyond all hope of reconstruction, for Europe houses the world's densest per capita concentration of nuclear targets, and much of the world's offensive nuclear weaponry. Recent talk of a nuclear war 'limited' to the European 'theatre', in which the USA and the eastern USSR would remain unscathed, underlines and heightens this danger. Europe is thoroughly 'stabilised' by the bloc system, and thoroughly 'defended' by a thirty-five year build-up of arms — which is now culminating in a balance of terror whose intensification, and indeed whose very maintenance, is an affront to reason and to the psychological welfare of the peoples of the continent.

It is unnecessary to dwell on the obstacles which confront pan-European movement of democratic anti-militarism: s are well aware of them, and particularly of the opposi- meets all forms of popular self-assertion in Eastern e of the detail of this problematic, hopeful and ive is discussed below (in chapter 2). Un- — the Europe of the Enlightenment and of the democratic strivings which have followed it, the Europe which has exported its civilisation along with its barbarism to so much of the globe — now finds itself faced with a historic peril, and a historic responsibility, lying as it does in what E.P Thompson has called 'the central locus of the opposed exterminist thrusts'.[5] European scientists and technicians, working within the framework of European capitalism, developed the technology of destruction which they refined (in an American programme) to its zenith/nadir of Hiroshima and Nagasaki. It would indeed be fitting if we could 'repay our debts to the world by engendering peace'.[6] The first step in our struggle, which will at once brighten our own immediate prospects and present our superpower captors with a truly 'modernised' definition of security, will be to rid our continent of weapons of mass destruction.

I am quite aware that this in itself will be no guarantee that we shall attain the goal of a disarmed world. We cannot guarantee our future (though we can be sure we shall not have one if we continue along our present path); and one need not be a defender of the nuclear status quo, as William Rodgers is, to acknowledge the perils which arise from the existing or emergent military nuclear capability of nations such as China, South Africa and India. We can, however, reject Mr Rodgers' hypocritical and lying claim that the two superpowers have used their 'best efforts' to restrain proliferation hitherto, when neither has done anything to implement Article VI of the Non-Proliferation Treaty, which calls upon them to begin negotiations for disarmament. But then Mr Rodgers appears to believe that the danger of proliferation is actually a reason why the nuclear weapon states should *not* disarm.[7]

It is obvious enough that if we wish to prevent the further spread of nuclear weapons the essential first step is to set up a massive momentum for genuine disarmament within the Soviet Union and the United States. Nothing will do more to create such a momentum than an unequivocal European demonstration that the stationing of nuclear arms in and around 'allied' territory today buys, not political subservience, but revolt. Europe has the economic power, the diplomatic weight, and — potentially — the transnational internal cohesion to mount an

12

effective resistance. If we can make it politically impossible for the superpowers to pile up their weaponry on European territory, we shall be working for superpower disarmament in a double sense: our leaders will be exerting diplomatic pressure on theirs, in concert with the hitherto relatively powerless non-aligned bloc (which includes Yugoslavia and Sweden as well as many Third World countries);[8] and our people will be urging the people of Russia and America to force upon their own political and military establishments a programme of disarmament which is plainly in the interests of Russian and American survival.

Once such a programme has been forced upon/taken up by the leadership of the superpowers, there is no reason to believe that it will be possible for lesser nations to continue developing their arsenals in defiance of what will then be effective, powerful and (for the first time) morally credible world opinion. Working in concert to contain what will then be, even more than it is today, a threat to their joint security, the Soviet and American leadership will be in a position to bring punitive economic pressure to bear upon recalcitrant states. Once committed to nuclear disarmament, the developed world would swiftly end its programme of exporting 'civil' nuclear technology — a technology which, apart from its intrinsic dangers and its very questionable performance, is ill-suited indeed to the energy needs of many of the importers, a number of whom (Iraq, Israel, India, Pakistan) at present obviously reserve the 'option' of developing its military applications. There would be an end, too, to the shameful export of arms to the poor world; and the military dictatorships which thrive worldwide on the export of violence, and the means of violence, would lose their current superpower support. Democratic insurgence, which is held in brutal check with the help of superpower (and above all Western) arms supplies, would be succoured in its struggle against racism and fascism. For only in a world where popular control is asserting itself in every national state will the manufacture and threatened use of weapons of mass destruction, which cannot be the weapons of self-governing peoples, begin to become inconceivable, until at last emancipated humanity can leave the nuclear age behind.

Such a world, it is unnecessary to insist, is hardly envisaged in the perspectives of imperialism. But unless imperialism and militarism are resisted from within the imperialist nations, and unless their aims are thwarted, there will be no world — no world, even, for capital to exploit. A 'utopian' international order such as I have sketched is also (to return to a theme of my opening paragraphs) a minimal necessity if humanity is to survive. Disarmament will bring in its train a quite different politics of coexistence — an end to the nonsense of 'peace through terror' (which has been no peace anyway in much of the poor world), and a beginning of peace through peace, peace because peace is what we want and must have.

Meanwhile, although we do not have many years in which to act, we have yet to take the first step. I have outlined this possible future only to insist that something of the kind *is* possible, and to counter the cynicism and defeatism of believers in perpetual (?) deterrence. But the focus of this book, which attempts a close and realistic look at immediate practical possibilities, is on the first, and still untaken step of nuclear disarmament.

More specifically, and although I have constantly tried to keep in mind the international, and particularly the European, dimension, its focus is on Britain. This is not just because it is primarily for British readers or because I am familiar with the British political scene and with discussions in British publications. It is also because of the unique position Britain occupies within Europe, within NATO and vis-a-vis the USA. It is not just that we possess an 'independent' deterrent (indeed, I devote little space to discussing this factor, an insignificant one in my view); nor that our country boasts a grotesquely heavy concentration of nuclear bases/targets, making us NATO's prime European airstrip or launching pad (and making nuclear disarmament an exceptionally desirable goal for the British people.[9] The aspect which is potentially of unique significance is the especially close relationship which binds us, as client state, to the American superpower — a relationship which is not simply one of military and economic subservience-dominance, but which involves ideological and sentimental elements which give it a particular political vitality. This is not a matter of our power or 'greatness' (delusions on that subject are endemic in Britain's military and political establishment); it is the result of a history whose force today is ambiguous, unpredictable. Nevertheless this same history might still lend weight to the actions of the British people, making the Pentagon and the White House, and American public opinion, highly responsive to a British foreign and defence policy which broke decisively with thirty-five years of nuclear subservience.

Such a policy can only begin with the taking of unilateral steps. In my own view (argued at length below, in chapter 3) Britain should close down all nuclear bases on its soil and in its waters. Any policy intended to put real political pressure on the USA must at the very least contain a refusal to accept cruise missiles here; and that refusal must be unconditional. It goes without saying that genuine multilateral disarmament would be preferable in every way. Indeed, multilateral disarmament would be the goal of such unilateral initiatives. Meanwhile the choice — the initial, practical choice — is not between unilateral and multilateral disarmament; it is between unilateral disarmament and no disarmament at all. Every nuclear state since Nagasaki (insofar as they have even acknowledged the need for disarmament at all) has claimed to favour a 'multilateral' approach, and has 'pursued' nuclear disarmament within that framework. Those who argue that this kind of diplomacy is suddenly going to produce real progress ignore the blatant evidence of history, and must be convicted either of naivety or of insincerity.

Thus the core of this book is a rehearsal, and a deepening, of the argument for British unilateral nuclear disarmament. This is certainly not conceived of as a 'gesture', made in isolation by a high-minded British government. It is conceived of as a measure forced upon the British state by intense popular agitation, and intended as an assertion of political independence vis-a-vis the USA and as a major contribution to an emerging European movement. And my argument (here and throughout) is intended *as* an argument — not an analysis tracing the factors which have engendered the weapons, nor a rhetorical protest against their existence, but a political argument which assembles evidence and debate, which proposes the possibility of acting in certain ways, and which tries to identify the forces we must defeat if we are to succeed.

I have tried to counter the arguments of those who would prefer Britain to retain its nuclear weapons, to welcome cruise missiles, and to accept forever the logic of deterrence on the grounds that 'the existence of nuclear weapons is a fact of life and we simply cannot wish them away'.[10] However (as this last phrase vividly indicates) the problem is not one of disagreement between people who share common premises, and accept the same framework of debate. The premises of every argument are chosen, they prefigure the conclusion, and since I am interested in another conclusion I begin from a different place. What is at issue, as in all political debate of a fundamental kind, is the framework itself. I hope to combat defeatism, and to convince readers that mine is a truer framework than that of the nuclear apologists — truer partly *because* it is more hopeful, for of what use is a 'realism' which leads into the abyss?

As well as convincing those who are unsure, this book is intended to speak to those who are already convinced, but who feel that they might enjoy, or benefit from, a broader and deeper consideration of the issues than has been undertaken in the many excellent pamphlets and essays that have been appearing over the last few months. It is a time for pamphlets and essays, and a tricky time for books, for events are moving swiftly. Much has changed since 'we' agreed to take our quota of Tomahawks, since E.P Thompson wrote *Protest and Survive*, since the END movement was launched, since the CND rally of October 1980; and much will no doubt change while this book is at the printer's. I have not tried to disguise the dependence of my argument, at this or that point, on the context of the moment; and events are sure to have overtaken me here and there. The underlying shape of the discussion, however, corresponds (I hope) to the underlying forces at play: on the one hand, the degenerative balance of terror and its 'logic of process', which leads, through this crisis and that resolution, towards the likelihood of nuclear war;[11] on the other hand, the movement of popular resistance, which has already achieved a good deal in Western Europe, which is gaining formidable strength in Britain, and whose continued growth and determination offer a real hope of survival.

1. Nuclear Weapons and Civilian Populations

Of all sectors of public spending, defence has suffered least from the present British government's monetarist policies. Housing, health and education have all been cut, but defence spending continues to rise, and will run at £12.3 billion in 1981-82. Nonetheless it is not rising fast enough to fulfil the promises made to the Services. Real resources cannot be stretched to meet unrealistic commitments, and the needs of 'economy' are causing disarray even in this lavishly funded area. In particular, the Trident programme, clearly seen as sacrosanct by this Cabinet, will siphon off a disproportionate share of the allocation. The general priority accorded to defence spending includes a specific, nuclear priority which risks distorting the entire shape of our already grandiose defences.[1]

Such priorities are not, however, chosen in sheer contempt of public opinion. Both the sum of money and the particular 'system' which will be the major drain on it reflect, and have been justified by, political and ideological consensus (although so far as Trident is concerned the programme does not in fact enjoy majority support).[2] Of course, official secrecy and deception, along with the compliance of the communications media, have helped maintain that consensus — which has in any case been a matter of passive acceptance rather than of enthusiastic commitment. The present major reopening of the issues has called in question assumptions which went unchallenged a few months ago: the consensual status quo has been fragile, based on silence (see chapter 4). But it can be particularly hard to contest 'opinions' not based on explicit reasoning; and when we discuss 'defence' it is clear that we are not dealing with ideas like those of monetarism or socialism, which are advocated as coherent rational constructions, but with feelings and beliefs rooted in our society. A nightclub owner gets some friends from the SAS to mount a 'raid' as an opening-night stunt; war films are the staple of the TV movie diet; a child's pyjama jacket is decorated with tanks and artillery amidst the sailing-boats and teddy bears; available Christmas 1980 was a new toy, *Apocalypse: the Game of Nuclear Devastation*. The means of annihilation, and their human operators, are heroes of our culture.

The complex of feelings and beliefs clustered around the idea of war owes something, no doubt, to pre-rational elements in the human psyche; something to the bitter routine competitiveness of modern life; something to imperial nostalgia, fading images of British greatness. Arguments in books will have little effect on factors such as these. But reasoned conceptions and historical experience also underlie ideas about security and defence, and for many Britons (including many politicians and military commanders) the experience of World War II, and the conceptions drawn from it, have a central importance here — just as recollections of the bravery and national solidarity which characterised that war continue to surround their idea of war in general with a positive emotional colouring.

If we reflect, however, on the events of 1939-45, we can see that they in fact call in question some of the ideas, especially about the relation between civilians and armed forces, which they may be thought to vindicate.

World War II and after: civilians and military

Britain's successful resistance to Hitler's armed forces might seem to confirm the premise of much thinking about defence — namely, the idea that the role of the military is to protect the civilian population against enemy aggression. To take the classic instance, if we think of the Battle of Britain, then it is indeed true that the inhabitants of London owed a great deal to the RAF: it was as well that the Spitfire was an effective fighter, and its crews brave and well trained. If war consists of battles such as this (in the air or on the ground), then civilians may hope to avoid defeat and its consequencs if their own units are sufficiently supplied and prepared. Security is thus best served — so the argument runs — by the maintenance of an ample fighting force provided with whatever weaponry technology has devised. Winston Churchill, MP, is fond of evoking those days, and urging his colleagues to rearm against Soviet might as their predecessors did too tardily against the Nazis. Implicit in his appeals is the old view that military might is the answer to military might, and that the people of Britain can be made secure by the building of a yet bigger arsenal.

If we could believe that a future war would be fought out between the armed forces of the combatant nations, such arguments would have more weight. If by investing in our own armoury we (the civilian population of Britain) could avoid exposure to that of our enemies, the investment would be well worth while. But it is in the nature of modern weapons, as World War II ought also to have taught us, that defence against them has become impossible. In 1939-45 this was already, and especially, true of aerial weapons: defensive measure were taken (radar surveillance, barrage balloons, anti-aircraft guns, the fighter planes mentioned above), but if sufficient bombers were sent, some always got through. The advantage lay inexorably with the aggressor; defensive action might limit casualties, but could no longer prevent them; and citizens (including babies, invalids, pacifists) were going to die, henceforth, however successfully their armed forces might fight back.

What, then, if the goal even of *limiting* civilian casualties should become unattainable? What if a bomb should be developed so powerful that just one could destroy a city? What if it should be deployed in such numbers that some were sure to reach their targets despite all counter-measures? Would not that render old conceptions of defence entirely obsolete?

As we know, the Allies were so concerned lest German scientists were developing such a bomb that they determined to pre-empt them. If the first large-scale bombing of civilians, at Guernica, was a profound shock, it was succeeded within a few years by events so traumatic that they will continue to haunt us until their repetition has been made impossible. In August 1945 first Hiroshima, and then Nagasaki, were destroyed by atomic weapons.

Those of course were early days, and indeed the Hiroshima bomb was known, with the disgusting flippancy of all such nomenclature, as 'Little Boy'. That 'puny and miserable weapon' (Mr Churchill's phrase)[3] killed only some 140,000 people at the time of its detonation. Today's weapons are very much 'improved', they exist in huge numbers, and their delivery systems have long since been refined to the point where our second hypothetical question — What if they were sure to reach their targets? — has been posed in actuality for many years now. As to whether previous conceptions of defence have been abandoned in consequence, they clearly have (in military minds), in the sense that reciprocal threat has frankly replaced any notion of defence in nuclear weapon states. This view of the matter, which is what 'deterrence' really means, is not often canvassed by our politicians, who understandably prefer to foster the naive view that our armed forces can still 'defend' us in the old sense.

Nonetheless most people now recognise that in any super-power war the civilian populations would stand little chance. This is not just because the deployment of nuclear weapons inevitably implies an ultimate strategy of mass mutual slaughter, which would be implemented in reality the moment the threat of it ('deterrence') failed. Even in the 'limited' war of the planners' fantasies, whose strikes would be aimed at military targets, some ten million Britons could expect to perish.[4] Should such a war break out in the European 'theatre', we may be sure that the dead soldiers, 'legitimate' targets, would be greatly outnumbered by the corpses of those whom they had set out to 'defend'.

To reiterate: the British people cannot be defended in the event of nuclear war. The same goes for the people of any other combatant nation. 'Our' military cannot protect us against 'theirs', but can only threaten in return. But these developments urge us to rewrite the definition of 'us' and 'them' (such a rewriting was long overdue). In considering modern war, and the 'defences' which prepare for it, we find ourselves paying less and less attention to the vertical divide between nation and nation, and more and more attention to the horizontal divide *within* each nation between civilians (common victims) and military (the common enemy). Such a view may be over-simple; it needs vindication and elaboration. It is not, for instance, simply a matter of who wears a military uniform. The Minister of Defence, the civil servants who service 'our' nuclear arsenal, the Prime Minister who might authorise the launching of Polaris missiles are all involved in the military apparatus, while common soldiers, in a nuclear war, would very likely share the fate — and indeed the feelings — of the population at large. Nor, of course, is this the only division in modern societies: other divisions of class and power, which also fall across national boundaries, parallel and in part engender this general separation between the state military apparatus and the civilians whom it 'protects'. But this general division, in the crude and obvious form which I have sketched, is there for all to see, and must exist in any nuclear weapon state, for it flows from the characteristics of the weapons themselves and can be traced everywhere in the strategies, the technologies, the ideology they breed — in the assumptions of strategic 'theorists' and Home Defence propagandists, and in the control systems of the weaponry itself.

Disarmament campaigners must emphasise this division, and develop the democratic and internationalist arguments which it prompts and which will help in the building of a movement strong enough to belie the apparent impotence of civilians.

Nuclear strategies

Since people cannot be protected against nuclear weapons, our security depends on ensuring that they are never used. One way to do this would be to abolish them, to recognise that peace must be maintained and strengthened, and to make the world a less volatile place by using the freed resources (over £200,000,000 was spent on arms in 1980) to combat poverty, disease and illiteracy. This rational programme has been endorsed by the UN Special Session on Disarmament, and it is the aim of the World Disarmament Campaign to mobilise support for such a strategy.

Meanwhile the governments of the nuclear weapon states have arranged a different 'security': the security of the balance of terror, of reciprocal threat, of Mutually Assured Destruction. They have mocked the hunger of millions, and the social aspirations of their own peoples, by devoting their best efforts to the refinement and marketing of death. The arms race continues to accelerate, while the existing nuclear stockpiles are already so destructive that many people have come to feel that war is inevitable — as E.M. Forster did in 1936, when he wrote that a world which piles up arms can no more help using them than a gorged animal can help discharging its filth.[5]

We must hope that it is too soon to speak of war as 'inevitable'. War undoubtedly will come if the arms race is not halted and reversed; and the arms race, for whose continuation there can be no semblance of rational excuse, is undoubtedly symptomatic of a profound social and historical crisis. We must recognise, however, that the deliberate initiation of a nuclear war would now and always will be an act of unparalleled folly, and that the strategy, or 'posture', of deterrence is primarily defensive, and embodies in perverse form the recognition that war *is* unthinkable. Nuclear Armageddon can never be a rational 'option', to which a beleaguered ruling class might turn, for no class and no state can profit by unleashing a power which would inevitably recoil upon and destroy its master. Armouries of unprecedented might involve an unprecedented impossibility of using them.

Nuclear missiles amount, in the familiar image, to pistols held at their launchers' heads. That said (and I am trying to characterise the uneasy 'peace' we now endure, the breathing-space with which we are presented), we can be rather more precise about whose heads the pistols are held against — and whose hands they are in. East and West, the missile bases are staffed and policed by military personnel, access is denied to the citizen, the control systems (even where they originate in a supposedly democratic polity) are in the hands of a very few. The targets, by contrast, can be found on every map: they are eminently visible and go by such names as Leningrad and Manchester. These two cities happen to be 'twinned': every year, for instance, twenty engineering apprentices come to the British city from its Soviet counterpart. No doubt their experiences confirm the truism that the lives of people everywhere have much in common, making it absurd for them to think of each other as mortal enemies. And yet deterrence means: if the citizens of Manchester (Leningrad) are massacred by the act of the military, the citizens of Leningrad (Manchester) will suffer the same fate in return.

Hostages have been much in the news of late, and it is quite accurate representation of deterrence to say that the civilian populations of the superpower blocs are held hostage, in their tens of millions, for the good behaviour of their military establishments. Certainly, this gives us the strongest possible interest in maintaining peace. Once that interest has been identified, however, we must surely find some means of safeguarding it more rational than the military 'solution' of endless threat and counter-threat (and indeed Manchester City Council, seeking to abjure that logic and its nuclear implements, has been a prime mover in the campaign to establish nuclear-free zones throughout Britain). The role of hostage begins to grow intolerable — we are unarmed, there is nowhere we can escape to, we doubt that our needs are being considered in the prestigious diplomatic charade which for years now has done nothing to restore our freedom or guarantee our survival. It is time, perhaps, to see if we are as powerless as we appear to think; time to try and take matters into our own hands.

The final strategy of deterrence — the threat of mass annihilation and mutual suicide, which would at once be realised should deterrence ever fail — itself provides overwhelming arguments for nuclear disarmament. Still, it is not incomprehensible that people have put their faith (if that can be the word) in this strategy, insofar as it has represented an acknowledgement that nuclear war is unthinkable, and has been designed to prevent it.[6] The resurgence of the disarmament movement has been in part a reaction to mutations in NATO strategy which have been plainly at *odds* with deterrence: 'limited' and 'theatre' war, 'counter-force' and 'first-strike' targeting, the planned deployment of cruise missiles.

The overriding general point about these new strategies (some of which, however, are by no means 'new')[7] is that they illustrate the truth — central to E.P. Thompson's argument in 'Protest and Survive'[8] — that deterrence must be a 'degenerative' and not a stationary state, for it has conferred an enormous power upon the military, so that military conceptions have come to determine political thinking, and specifically thinking about, precisely, arms and disarmament. Deterrence, in terms of its own 'pure' logic, requires no new weapons programmes, no new strategies; indeed such developments undermine its very basis. And yet the military, exerting the influence they have gained, continue to build up arsenals to levels at which the consequences of any failure or miscalculation grow ever more appalling, and at which the simple equation of minimum deterrence is lost to sight amidst the proliferation of 'usable' and 'flexible' nuclear weapons.

As for the strategic mutations themselves, the relevant issues have been incisively discussed, and I shall not rehearse them here.[9] These strategies are in fact so plainly irrational that even the military establishment can hardly believe they could be implemented without inevitable MAD (the nuclear strategists' acronym for Mutually Assured Destruction). The British Ministry of Defence, for instance, now explains that cruise missiles are useless as first strike weapons (they would be too slow),[10] thus disavowing the scenario which makes most 'sense' of their technical specification... And yet we must not forget that the new weapons are being built, while evidence is continually coming to light that the fantasy of 'limited war' is being allowed to influence contingency planning — which now envisages the airlifting of 100,000 casualties from a European nuclear war to specially reserved beds in US hospitals.[11]

These mutations also make visible the mechanisms which force the arms race insanely upwards within the collapsing 'stability' of deterrence. First of all, it is to be noted that the cruise missile has been on the drawing-board for many years,[12] and was deliberately left unaffected by the SALT provisions. The American arms industry has its own momentum, it is a vested interest of remarkable and tenacious influence, and from this point of view the 'doctrine' of counter-force amounts merely to a retrospective 'justification' for the manufacture and purchase of a new commodity. Such commodities, moreover, clearly appeal to a military establishment equipped for years now with grotesque nuclear overkill, whose prestige, and the psychic needs of whose personnel, nonetheless depend upon the acquisition of still more weapons of mass destruction. If the 'need' for such weapons, accurate enough to land on a tennis court the far side of a continent, can only be conjured out of a strategy which ignores the reality of assured destruction in favour of perilous nonsense about 'war-fighting' and 'limited options', that is too bad: the nonsense will have to be enshrined in Presidential Directives, the happy compliance of the Soviet bureaucracy in modernising their own 'theatre forces' will be invoked (quite dishonestly)[13] as the justifying *quo* for NATO's *quid*, and the people of Western Europe will have to be persuaded to acquiesce.

The reality, fortunately, is turning out rather different. The strategies are not being left to the strategists, and the question of cruise missiles is not being contested in the terms of the nuclear games-rooms. The military and political establishment, and their allies in the Press and on TV, are finding the language in which they have fortified each other and tried to soothe the rest of us pushed aside in favour of quite another discourse, which asks (about cruise missiles, and then about all nuclear weapons), not, Do they strengthen NATO, do they fit into 'our' latest strategy? but, Do they make us safer, and how are we to get rid of the whole arsenal? Questions of the second kind, though plainly of the highest importance for the future of humanity, have of course always been regarded as closed or hopelessly naive in official circles. But that only underlines the degree to which the needs and fears of civilians are being ignored in our increasingly militarised world.

Home Defence: 'acceptable damage'?

The issue of Home Defence, though in a sense peripheral to the larger question of arms and disarmament, has played a big part in the recent growth of public consciousness about nuclear weapons. Most people do realise the futility of the advice contained in *Protect and Survive*, and know that they will perish in a nuclear attack; but home defence arrangements continue to attract attention.[14] This is entirely understandable, since nuclear war would mean a peculiarly horrible death for many millions of people, and it is this disturbing truth which is irresistibly highlighted by the very 'arrangements' which attempt to hide it from us.

A less publicised, but most revealing, aspect of the plans lies in their frank totalitarianism. The authority of the state would be the sole 'social structure' to survive a nuclear war, and *Square Leg* — the big 'home defence' exercise of September 1980 — showed how this authority would be imposed: *Socialist Worker* published a document listing army and police functions, the first nine of which are exclusively concerned with 'problems' of social control ('support and protect special courts', 'execution of sentences', 'personal protection for VIPs', and so on).[15] Such planning is consistent with the selective survival strategy which funnels most Home Defence funds into the building of secret bunkers and command-posts, to which the ordinary citizen and her/his children need expect no invitation. What is still more disturbing is the extent to which totalitarian conceptions colour the establishment view of the 'pre-attack period', with anti-war demonstrators ('pacifism as a front for subversion') rounded up by troops, the internment of radicals and left-wingers ('Red Peace Trotskyists'), HMG suspending parliament and devolving its authority to unelected regional and county controllers, and cabinet ministers retiring with military chiefs to guarded hide-outs where they can plan their next move undisturbed by such protesters as may have eluded the attentions of F6 (the Home Office department responsible for the control of subversive elements in a nuclear emergency).[16] These plans have obvious implications (to which I return below) for whoever wants to resist nuclear annihilation: resistance must begin *now*. They encourage a certain scepticism as to the kind of 'freedom' which a nuclear war would turn out to have 'defended': and it is instructive to note that our democracy, as perceived by those whom it has put in power (and by their civil servants), already allows such plans to be concocted.

This is the aspect of Home Defence which should be taken at face value — and which we are not intended to glimpse. Most Whitehall politicians actually believe, or at any rate feel obliged to pretend, that nuclear war would be preferable to surrender: 'as much as we hate the horror of nuclear war... our values and principles would have to be defended'.[17] Therefore they must make plans for it and, since no population would be led unresisting into suicide, those plans must specifically aim to prevent pre-attack 'subversion' (mass pressure for surrender) and to ensure that power would remain firmly in the hands of the state.

What cannot be taken at face value is the advice given to ordinary people. I need offer no critique of *Protect and Survive*, both because others have ably done so,[18] and because the document reveals its own absurdity ('on hearing the all-clear, you may resume normal activities'). Nonetheless it is worth insisting that this document, printed (by a Labour government, incidentally) at some public expense, is deliberately, and doubly, deceptive. It is deceptive in the specific sense that its stay-put advice, useless for anyone within the zones of blast and fire and for many miles downwind, very plainly reduces — and must thus be *intended* to reduce — the immediate survival chances of those in the numerous military and industrial target areas. It is deceptive, too, in the general sense that it ignores the weight of medical and scientific evidence indicating that 'effective civil defence against a nuclear attack is impossible' and that 'under all conditions, medically, nuclear war would be an unparalleled catastrophe'.[19] Its function is ideological, and the ideology is for our consumption. We are to be persuaded that the appropriate response to the nuclear threat is not to work for disarmament, but to decide how best to 'protect' ourselves and our children — whether beneath a table in the basement or in an expensive custom-built shelter.

This is not to say that all advocates of Home Defence are conscious hypocrites. Tory backbenchers who enthuse over a death-toll 'reduced' to 20 million, professionals such as Sir Leslie Mavor (who has said that his work at the Easingwold Home Defence College would be vindicated if even a few *thousand* Britons survived)[20] — men like these may be quite well-intentioned. They do not gloat over the unutterable catastrophe; they simply see it as a potential consequence of a military strategy which remains, for them, beyond discussion. Of course the military strategy *must* be discussed, and changed; but those who evade the question may do so out of blindness rather than wickedness. All the same, I have felt at times a sinister kinship between the advocates of Home Defence and the Top Brass of World War I, in whose eyes 'the men', however sincerely esteemed and lamented, remained first of all *expendable*. Brighton Councillor Ian McGill, former Labour group leader and an *ex officio* member of the District Emergency Committee, has noted that those most zealous to 'protect' us are often drawn from the same High Tory milieu whose values of class privilege, militarism and outdated patriotism are so well represented in the upper echelons of the Services.[21] People like these are participating, whether 'well-meaningly' or otherwise, in plans which, for most of us, can only be plans for our non-survival. If we are called upon to make the great sacrifice in defence of our 'values and principles', the decision will be strictly military, and our role as civilians will be that of helpless targets. No amount of Home Defence propaganda can obscure that grim reality.

Here, undoubtedly, is an excellent focus of campaigning. The question of defence policy is brought down to local level, for county and borough authorities are supposed to take part in Home Defence exercises (the refusal of many to do so is part of the growing nuclear-free zones movement).[22] An opportunity is given to remind, or inform, people of the immense destructive power of thermonuclear weapons. The duplicity of the government is shown up, as is the divide between 'them' and 'us' — the theme of this chapter, and an essential dimension of the nuclear disarmament argument.

Still, disarmers should be careful not to get trapped in a debate whose currency is base. How much does it matter, in the end, whether ten thousand or ten million Britons would 'survive' a nuclear war? Human civilisation would not in any case have survived — it would have suffered a blow from which it could never recover. To think that we might find ourselves in some kind of 'medieval' society is to forget that those times, for all their barbarity, produced Giotto's painting, the poetry of Dante and Chaucer. Such affirmations could have no place in whatever 'culture' emerged from the holocaust. It is not perverse to stress these themes. If we think only of the destruction of tractors, dams, factories, and if we frame our argument in terms of mere physical survival, we are already admitting a defeat, and succumbing to brutal military conceptions which see human life as a bare choice between existence and annihilation. The choice today is still wide open. We can still work for a future which nuclear war would make forever unattainable.

Control systems

US Secretary of State Dean Rusk once said that: 'the danger of war by accident...grows as modern weapons become more complex, command and control difficulties increase, and the premium is on ever-faster reaction.'[23] The only comfort to be drawn from his words lies in the fact that they were spoken as long ago as 1962. We are still here. In the interim, there have been a number of false alarms. The series of computer-generated alerts which three times put US nuclear forces on a war footing in 1979 and 1980 was one factor in the rebuilding of the disarmament campaign.

These alarms may of course have been deliberately publicised, as part of a Cold War propaganda crescendo. It is hardly credible — to look a few years ahead — that the American military should entrust the survival of the world to the pieces of wire and micro-chips which, in the planned 'launch-on-warning' system, will replace possible human intervention.[24] And yet what is 'human intervention', when human beings must in any case rely on data from computerised electronic surveillance systems? The folly of 'launch-on-warning', manifest as it is, nonetheless fits quite well into a certain technical rationale, which is itself the acknowledgement of the 'premium' on 'ever-faster reaction' — a 'premium' which grows higher as the strategy, and weaponry, of 'first-strike' and 'counter-force' are introduced, inducing a mounting, and 'rational', paranoia in those responsible for ballistic missile arsenals which become ever more vulnerable to pre-emption. After all, the momentum of technical 'progress' long ago swept aside reason and true security, which can now be salvaged only by disarmament, by politically enforced technical 'regression'.

Meanwhile, various categories of 'accident' are possible. Malfunction is endemic to complex electronic circuitry. A catastrophic nuclear weapons accident might kill millions, and might lead to all-out war through the mistaken belief that it was part of a deliberate enemy attack. Political miscalculation, especially in a time of great tension or military confrontation, might lead one side to launch its missiles in the mistaken and despairing conviction that the other side had made up its mind to do so. None of these possibilities is much canvassed by defenders of the deterrent status quo, for none of them can be presented as rational. This is an issue on which disarmament campaigners should strive to focus public attention, for the danger of such accidents may be greater than that of a deliberate nuclear strike, or even of deliberate military confrontation between the superpowers. Not only that: the constant presence of this danger, its plain unbearable absurdity, betrays the absurdity of the 'deterrence' which engenders it. For deterrence is, precisely, the ever-present readiness to launch the nuclear arsenal, which maintains the constant threat of mutual annihilation/suicide.

Quite apart from its intrinsic perils, the nuclear 'control system' is frighteningly *beyond* control, for it consists, and must consist, of a technical network operated by a tiny elite, itself subject only to such 'political' discipline as resides in the say-so of Presidents (who in a 'retaliatory' strike would in any case merely authorise a decision already taken, on false or true information, by the military-technical apparatus). Of course, human agents are involved lower down the hierarchy (although their agency would be null, for obedience to commands is the virtue which must distinguish them): the missile systems have their 'key turners', who are not just rational, but screened for mental health. Their 'healthy' attitude to the weapons they must be ready to launch is well demonstrated by the fact that the fridges in their mess rooms are adorned with stickers reading 'Minutemen have more thrust' (the Minuteman is an ICBM with a warhead about twenty-five time as destructive as the Hiroshima bomb).[25]
    All this, clearly, has nothing whatever to do with any notion of democratic control. Not only is the mass of the civilian population the inevitable target of nuclear missiles, it also inevitably finds itself deprived of control over their launching. Once again we see the divide running through the nuclear-armed state which enforces our status as hostages in military hands. Who can doubt that in any 'pre-attack period', whether this lasted days or hours, thousands of people would struggle to wrest 'control' of the 'system' back into their own hands, or that this struggle would be futile? If we are to die in a nuclear war, some of our last and bitterest reflections will bear upon

our impotence.

Such reflections would hardly be sweetened by the knowledge that those who did have control would stand the best chance of survival. Common soldiers would not last long, perhaps, for all their protective gear; but the missile commanders in Cheyenne Mountain would shelter beneath solid granite; like their political confederates, they would have filtered air, supplies of food and water; and the High Command, in Europe as in the USA, would take off in flying control rooms. They would have a fine view of the destruction they had wrought.[26] Maybe there are Soviet equivalents to these flying control rooms, guarded with their own phalanx of fighter planes, and perhaps if the Strato-Kremlin chanced to pass within view of the Aero-Pentagon above a devastated Europe the respective crews, in a quaint survival of diplomatic protocol, would refrain from hostile action and exchange salutes instead. For the relative immunity of the Top Brass is among the oldest, as it is among the most instructive, of military traditions. What has changed is the scale on which today's generals are preparing to sacrifice their victims.

What has also changed is the nature of those victims' possible resistance, which cannot, in the modern world, assert itself at the penultimate moment. The 'control system' which deprives *us* of control also shortens the time-span between 'penultimate' and 'ultimate' to a matter of a few minutes.

Resistance to nuclear war

In persuading its citizens to wage a 'conventional' war, any state confronts a double problem. At home, an ideological, political and economic structure must be maintained to ensure that weapons can be manufactured and conscripts enlisted, and that internal opposition will not sabotage the war effort by way of industrial action, rioting, and so on. On the battlefield, disaffection must be smothered and discipline maintained among the troops. This offers dissenters two modes or phases of resistance: campaigns of political opposition, conscientious objection and draft evasion can disrupt domestic preparations, and soldiers can desert or show 'cowardice' or recalcitrance. America's war in Vietnam ended as it did, not only because of the tenacity of the Vietnamese people, but also because the Pentagon lost the political battle at home, while the troops became increasingly demoralised and mutinous.

A nuclear war would offer no such possibilities of resistance. For all the insistence on our need to amass a huge conventional armoury for the defence of Europe, any crossing of the line between the territories of NATO and of the Warsaw Pact would almost certainly lead to nuclear war within a few days (in the 1980 *Square Leg* exercise, the nuclear strike came on the fifth day of hostilities).[27] There would be no question of conscription or of conscientious objection; and political opposition to the war would have little prospect of success, given the inaccessibility of the control systems and the massive internal security operation which would be mounted. The government, secure in guarded bunkers, could in any case ignore a general strike, or even an insurrection, since it would only need to maintain its 'authority' for a few days, during which the complete collapse of the social and economic order would be a temporary inconvenience — and a mild foretaste of the post-nuclear struggle between anarchy and totalitarianism.

Thus the important question, for the nuclear-armed state, is not whether it can persuade its citizens to *fight* a nuclear war. Obviously it could not do so, 'when the crunch came', for surrender would be preferable. But our assent would be superfluous, for our role (as targets) would be enforced. The real question, for state and citizens alike, is whether we — we, for instance, in this country — are ready to participate in the *preparations* which make such a war a British 'option' (and make Britain a target in such a war). Hitherto, the answer to that question has been Yes. Come some future crisis, some further 'heightening of international tension', there will be no chance of turning that 'Yes' into a 'No'. Effective resistance has to begin now, while it still stands some chance of success.

This means that it cannot take the form of resistance to this or that particular possibility of war. Abstracting from specific 'scenarios', it can only — and must — challenge the setting of the stage itself, and press for the removal of the weapons which make extinction likely. That challenge — which may seem naive, in a world whose sophisticated strategists can produce any number of 'hideous worst cases',[28] and which certainly cannot be squared with a narrowly nationalistic conception of security — is strengthened by arguments which address the consequences of nuclear 'defence' *wherever* it is adopted. I have been outlining one such set of arguments, which point to the oppression of the civilian population entailed by nuclear strategies, and which pose the questions in an international and democratic, rather than a merely national, perspective. It is part of these arguments that they insist on our powerlessness in the event of war, and show how little control we have even today over the means of our 'defence'. But we must not fall into the error of believing that we (the civilian population, the great mass of the people) are *really* impotent, so that it is all someone else's fault. Our arguments and our tactics have to grasp this double paradox: we are *responsible* for a situation in which we seem *deprived* of responsibility; and if we wish to reclaim our power, we can only do so by asserting, and showing, that we *already have it*.

2. Nationalism, Internationalism and European Nuclear Disarmament

The initiative for European Nuclear Disarmament (END) aims to fuse together movements against nuclear weapons throughout Europe. END activists do not intend to see the movement succumb to the inertia of diplomatic negotiations as these have hitherto been conducted. They mean to build a framework within which moves by different peoples and governments can develop a common momentum, and thus to transcend the false dichotomy between a unilateralism which is derided as 'unrealistic'[1] and the multilateral diplomacy which has achieved nothing whatever in the disarmament field, and precious little in terms of arms control.

The general question of multilateralism and unilateralism is discussed in the next chapter. Here, I want to outline the case (as I see it) for European nuclear disarmament, and to examine some of the difficulties which will confront a movement working for a common programme across a continent riven by the East-West divide. For, quite apart from considerable divergences *within* the blocs (compare France with Norway, or Romania with Czechoslovakia), conditions obviously differ between the two 'sides' — this applies to social and political structures, to the stationing of weapons, and to the different military and diplomatic strategies of the dominant superpowers. These different conditions will inevitably present the END movement with delicate tactical and political decisions. It has already been criticised, from right and left, because of its insistence on arguing for common action in East and West: Conor Cruise O'Brien accuses E.P. Thompson of ignoring Soviet repressiveness, while John Cox (in a more sympathetic spirit) suggests that the END Appeal, in which the movement's initiators outlined its programme and invited public support, resorts to 'transparent even-handedness' where it might frankly have recognised the greater militarism of NATO.[2]

Such criticisms, and others,[3] have their validity, and I shall try to reply to them. But an essential point which many critics miss, and which must be stressed at the outset, is that END seeks to place the political questions, and decisions, in a new framework — the framework not of diplomacy dominated by the superpowers, but of popular sentiment, opinion and action. Here, 'popular' also, and crucially, means 'transnational'. It is not just that END will get nowhere, and recognises that it will get nowhere, unless it 'wins the support of multitudes';[4] it is also necessary for this movement to be unprecedentedly inter-nationalist — in philosophy, practice and support; a living embodiment of the democracy and internationalism which are inextricably linked in today's disarmament movement. The strategy which follows from this internationalism will not content itself with appealing to negotiators. It must instead mount a challenge within each nation state and group of states against the politics of superpower dominance and the weapons that sustain that politics.

It is very plain that such challenges can much more easily be mounted in the relatively open and democratic societies of Western Europe than they can in the East. This is the fundamental problem for the END strategy, and needs to be considered in detail. It involves, moreover, the intertwining of political and military factors which will complicate our discussion at every turn. Meanwhile, in these introductory remarks, I should like to clarify two points. The first is military-geographical, and concerns the current disposition within Europe of nuclear weapons; the second has to do with the broader political objective which is envisaged as the long term goal, and effect, of European nuclear disarmament.

There is a fundamental asymmetry in the geographical distribution of nuclear weapons. Western Europe harbours many thousand nuclear warheads, but it is widely thought that relatively few, if any, are permanently deployed in the satellite nations of the Soviet bloc.[5] In that sense, those nations are *already* as much 'nuclear-free zones' as is, say, Norway — which like them has no nuclear weapons deployed on its territory, although facilities exist which would allow them to be moved there in the event of actual or anticipated military confrontation. In seeking a nuclear-free zone 'from Poland to Portugal',[6] END has as its first goal the removal of all arms stationed in the political territory of Europe — and might to that extent appear to aim at 'unilateral' nuclear disarmament by the Western bloc. But this would be no more than a first step, which would have to be followed by a phasing out of all facilities, East and West, which allow nuclear weapons to be readily transported into and deployed within Europe. Beyond that, both superpowers would have to be obliged to respect the nuclear inviolability of the disarmed zone; and in particular, the USSR would have to remove from European Russia the nuclear arsenal now stationed there, get rid of the SS-20s targeted on Europe, and thus accept the wider definition of the zone: 'from the Urals to the Atlantic Ocean'.[7] In reality, if the campaign succeeds, these phases will probably not appear as chronologically distinct, but will be merged in a common process fusing together popular international (and unilateralist) pressure for disarmament, the assertion of autonomy by client states within the blocs, and enforced (and genuine) bilateral negotiations between the USSR and the USA.

As for the political objective envisaged alongside END's explicit military, or anti-militarist, goal, this has been indicated by E.P. Thompson:

> There has been, for 30 years, a build-up not only of weaponry but of antagonistic ideologies. The division of Europe is now accepted as an irrevocable fact of nature.
>
> [END] challenges not only the weapons but this 30-year-old fact.

And the form and tactics of this challenge have been sketched, again by Thompson, as follows:

> The rising movement in Western Europe against NATO 'modernisation' must exact a real price from the Soviet ideologists and military managers, in the opening of Eastern Europe to genuine exchanges and to participation in the common internationalist discourse. This must not be a hidden tactic but an open and principled strategy.[8]

END seeks, by establishing communication and solidarity across the East-West divide, not just to support democratic initiatives in the East, but to open new political possibilities in the whole of Europe.

It might of course be preferable if we could heed the fears of Dr Freedman, and keep the matter of 'the bomb' neatly distinct from the matter of 'fundamental political change in Europe on either side of the iron curtain'.[9] In the real world which we unfortunately inhabit, such compartmentalisation is, however, impossible. In the first place, it hardly seems likely, after all this time, that we shall rid ourselves of 'the bomb' unless we create some 'fundamental political change'. In the second place, the degenerative nature of the balance of terror is nowhere more evident than in its paralysing effect upon European politics. The ideological war which is part of 'deterrence' has allowed the ruling classes in both blocs to outlaw and marginalise movements of radical opposition by identifying them with the ('imperialist' or 'marxist') enemy without. This is more flagrant, and its consequences far more brutal, in the East; it will be the 'justification', already publicly rehearsed, for any Soviet 'intervention' against the Polish workers' movement. But we hear it nearer home too: socialists in the Labour Party are accused of wanting to transform cosy 'pluralist' (capitalist) Britain into 'an Eastern European regime'. Meanwhile the dole queues of Newcastle, as well as the food queues of Gdansk, bespeak the need for change.

The struggle to free Europe from nuclear weapons and from the immediate threat of extinction in a 'theatre war' is also, and consciously, a struggle to renew progressive forces, East and West. The kinds of national society and European community which those liberated forces may create can only be envisaged in general terms. Suffice it to say, here, that nothing has more perniciously affected Europe's political culture than the double (and doubly false) equation: 'socialism = authoritarianism', 'capitalism = freedom'. If END succeeds, that might lead in time to a cutting of this double knot. Perhaps Europeans might establish, authentically, the equation 'socialism = freedom' — a different socialism, a different freedom, than any we know today.

But the first step of disarmament is still to be taken. In arguing for it, let me begin with an observation at once banal and absurd: although the peoples of Europe have no desire to make war on one another, the nations of Europe are equipped as never before for mutual annihilation.

Nationalism and internationalism in Europe

The equipment of annihilation, nuclear and conventional, is in place, and if the 'official scenario' of such military fantasies as *Operation Crusader*, the NATO exercise of autumn 1980, is ever realised, it will be used, and Europe will be devastated. That much is clear. What is open to debate is my contention that Europe is not riven by hostility — internal, *European* hostility — such as would of itself make war likely. I do not claim that the continent is free of economic, national and ideological tensions. What I do claim — and this is the basis of END's internationalism — is that Europe is in peril, not because of such tensions, but because of the hostility of the superpowers, who parcelled out the continent at the end of the World War II, whose interest underlies and who assiduously promote the one really fundamental ideological division in Europe, and whose weaponry constitutes the major threat to the lives of Europeans. END aims to mobilise and to express a transnational solidarity which is at once a response to that threat and a means by which it may be dispelled. In the words of the END Appeal:

> We must commence to act as if a united, neutral and pacific Europe already exists. We must learn to be loyal, not to 'East' or 'West', but to each other, and we must disregard the prohibitions and limitations imposed by any national state.[10]

It is of course possible to smile at this exhortation, to mock its vision of 'the peoples of the continent recognising their common humanity, *stripped of nationalist blinkers*'.[11] We know Europe's recent history, we have not forgotten the national and racial hysteria of Hitler's nazism. Why should we think that things are different today, or believe that European consciousness has undergone a fundamental change?

Changes in consciousness, let us remind ourselves, are first of all responses to altered material realities. No one (for instance) lived in fear of the nuclear holocaust in 1500. And the existence of nuclear weapons must itself have helped to weaken militaristic nationalism. Nationalist aggression, of the kind fomented by Hitler and a host of earlier leaders, recruits its servants, military and civilian, by a promise of victory. But to contemplate nuclear war is to confront, at the very moment of contemplation, the emptiness of that promise, and to know in advance the outcome which has in truth always awaited the people of warring nations — an outcome of slaughter, destruction and misery in which people everywhere are too plainly the losers. Those who believe that human mutual slaughter is 'natural' or 'inevitable' give too little weight to the fact that war, which depends on the compliance of human beings, is profoundly irrational from their standpoint. Human beings are irrational too — in part; and nationalist ideologies have reflected, and expoited, their unreason. But they are capable of reason too: and the twentieth century, which in so many ways demands the assertion of human and rational control over mankind's social and technical creations, above all demands, and promotes, a recognition that this 'eternal' crime and folly of war can go on no longer, and a mobilisation of international popular resistance against the national ideologies and machines of genocide which make it still possible. Europe — because it has been the site of such bitter mutual destruction, and because its peoples know they can never go down that road again — is a place where such a mobilisation might begin.

Post-war Europe, too, has seen a host of concrete quotidian developments which undermine the ignorance and suspicion which provide nationalism's ideological basis. Tourism, the twinning of towns and cities, artistic and cultural contacts, the European Cup, instantaneous electronic communications — these, alongside economic and diplomatic cooperation, have brought Europeans together, not only within the superpower blocs, but across the 'iron curtain' also. It would not be easy to dress up in uniform the busdrivers and schoolteachers of Cracow and Amsterdam, transport them to distant battlefields, and have them massacre one another.

Such a war, it will be said, is not envisaged. Precisely: what is envisaged is a war caused and controlled by a military and political elite, itself dominated by non-European 'allies'; a war which the people of Europe will not have wished to fight, but in which their cooperation will be unnecessary, for they will be called upon merely as targets, the hapless inhabitants of a convenient (to whom?) 'theatre'. This is just why we must push back the missiles, and assert that in our eyes Europe is, and shall remain, a theatre of peace.

Once we adopt a European perspective, there is an irresistible argument for ridding the continent of the nuclear overkill currently targeted upon its people in the cause of their 'protection'. But even when it has won massive support among Europeans, the argument will not carry the day of itself in the Kremlin and the Pentagon, whose 'protection' has been much like that offered by thugs and gangsters: it has had little to do with guaranteeing our security, but a lot to do with enforcing our allegiance to whichever Power we have entrusted with our 'defence'.

The USA and the USSR: global conduct and European arms balance

The thoughts voiced in the preceding paragraphs express a European, and explicitly neutralist, view. It is by no means the only view, for the 'mutual and collusive'[12] strategies of the superpowers have their own rationales, endorsed by European political leaders within the alliances which they respectively dominate, and hitherto accepted, or at any rate tolerated, by the populations of those alliances. It is these rationales which we must now criticise and compare.

This will inevitably involve us in other, highly vexed, comparisons: the overall comparison between the military and foreign policies of the two superpowers, and the specific question of the European balance of arms. These topics cannot be avoided, for they provide the context within which apologists for the status quo invariably frame their arguments.

On the question of global strategy and conduct, I should like to quote again from the END Appeal:

> We do not wish to apportion guilt between the political and military leaders of East and West. Guilt lies squarely on both parties. Both parties have adopted menacing postures and committed aggressive actions in different parts of the world.[13]

It is true that this phraseology might seem 'equivocal', in that it does not say that guilt lies *equally* on both parties, and yet refuses to say where it lies the heavier. But this (probably deliberate) 'equivocation' is, in my view, quite justified. Once we begin to compare the worldwide actions of the superpowers (leaving aside their respective social systems), we see over the years a series of 'interventions' — overt and covert, military, paramilitary, economic, political: Hungary, Czechoslovakia, Afghanistan, Vietnam, Chile, El Salvador... Reasonable men and women may well differ as to which superpower has a 'better' (or worse) record. They may well reject altogether a calculus which invites them to trade off the crushing of democracy in Eastern Europe against the immolation of South-East Asian peasants. The crucial point, surely — and here, precisely, the Appeal is *not* equivocal — is that *both* superpowers have behaved in ways which oblige us to condemn them *both*. This is not to say that we cannot form a relative judgement — though this is unlikely to be a simple one ('A is better than B'), since the actions to be compared, and their motivations, are heterogeneous.[14] What we cannot do is to base the argument for European nuclear disarmament on a position which is simply *pro* either superpower. Western peace campaigners who echo Soviet propaganda, claim that all Russian missiles are purely defensive, and endorse the entire record of Soviet foreign policy, can have no more place in the campaign than those Eastern dissidents who believe that the USA and her allies are the pure champions of freedom, regard cruise missiles as a legitimate defence of Western Europe, and echo The Voice of America.[15]

This refusal to identify either superpower with the cause of 'peace' is enforced by the discipline of facts. It is also necessary to the form of our argument, its specifically European logic. The hostility of the superpowers is also a collusion; it must be challenged by a movement from outside that fatal pairing. Our arguments must begin from another place, or they will inevitably become entangled in the 'logic' of justification/recrimination which confirms the leaders, and the peoples, of the USA and the USSR in the nuclear embrace in which they are currently leading each other, and themselves, towards oblivion.

The question of the European military balance is made 'controversial' mainly by the success of the propaganda campaign launched by the NATO apologists to convince us that we need a new 'generation' of weaponry. Those who wish to present a more balanced view have to challenge the formidable, but quite erroneous, 'consensus' created by those apologists, whose 'facts' and arguments are based on a familiar blend of misinformation, disinformation and deceit. Entire categories of arms have been taken out of the nuclear equation (British Polaris missiles, US Poseidon warheads, bombs aboard F-111 and Vulcan bombers, the 'European' arsenal carried on US aircraft carriers), and the designations of 'theatre' and 'medium-range' weapons have been arbitrarily determined, in order to demonstrate a Soviet preponderance.[16] Cruise missiles, the MoD explains, will allow a 'controlled and precise' response... with 200 kiloton warheads![17] The neutron bomb is officially advocated as an anti-tank weapon, although modern precision guided weapons perform that role very well,[18] do not have the side effect of killing every living thing for hundreds of yards, and would not risk inducing a 'controlled' response, but at a slightly less 'precise' level, which would then lead through stages of escalation to an all-out war. And this rigged nuclear argument is then underpinned by the interminably reiterated assertion of an overwhelming Warsaw Pact advantage in conventional arms.

This tissue of distortions has been patiently unravelled by such writers as Mary Kaldor and (especially) Dan Smith, with whose work activists in the disarmament movement should be conversant.[19] Without reproducing their discussion in detail, we can summarise its conclusions. So far as the European nuclear balance is concerned, it is very hard to make out a case for Soviet superiority — and quite impossible to do so on a global basis (a most important point if we consider, as I do, that the nuclear confrontation in Europe is essentially an effect, or component, of the global confrontation). So far as the conventional balance is concerned, it is enough to say that the International Institute of Strategic Studies (by no stretch of the imagination an anti-NATO body) concludes that there is a rough parity of forces.[20]

A further, and important, point also needs to be made. If

the discussion is about European 'theatre' nuclear weapons, it cannot be too often insisted that all talk about the 'need' for more of these is contemptibly irrational (and this of course applies to the SS-20 just as it does to cruise missiles and neutron bombs). Our continent already has targeted upon its military installations, industrial centres and cities a nuclear arsenal sufficient to destroy its civilisation and kill most of its inhabitants many times over.

Even within Europe there are, however, as we have noted, advocates of this contemptible unreason. The European strategies of the superpowers are regularly presented as defensive — defensive, not only of the legitimate interests of the superpowers, but of the territorial integrity and national autonomy of the client states.

'Freedom' and 'socialism' defended:
Europe through American and Russian eyes

The rationales for the European strategies of the superpowers are in many respects mirror-images. Both rationales are maintained, not only to justify the status quo, but to legitimise the introduction of perilous 'new generations' of nuclear missiles. Both the USA and the USSR take it that the threat which they think each poses to the other's existence is best countered by the deployment of massive overkill (a response, of course, which maintains and intensifies the state of increasingly *real* threat). Beneath this interlocking arch of 'deterrence', Europe is seen as a particularly clearly defined area of 'coexistence', its stability assured by the system of military blocs. Meanwhile — reverting for a moment to the European perspective — that explicitly defensive bloc system is also the means by which superpower hegemony is covertly guaranteed: in the East, by frank military enforcement; in the West, by the deployment of nuclear weapons which, it is clear, increasingly supplements, and to an extent replaces, the economic strength by which the USA has hitherto dominated Western Europe.

This rough balance or reciprocity is, however, complicated by a geographical *im*balance which is perceived differently in the Kremlin and in the Pentagon: the USA lies on the far side of the Atlantic, but much of the Soviet Union is within continental Europe. The differing significance accorded to this immutable geographical imbalance introduces an element of fundamental difference into superpower (and superpower bloc) perceptions of the European 'theatre'.

We in the West are very familiar with the NATO perception. We are daily reminded that Soviet tanks could in principle drive all the way from the Polish border to the Cap de la Hague nuclear power station. Against this threat — so we are told — Western Europe alone is powerless. Our security can only be guaranteed by an alliance with the sole world power capable of matching Russian might; and such an alliance must accept the 'option' of possible nuclear first use, given what is generally (if dubiously) presented as an overwhelming Soviet non-nuclear superiority. To disband the European bloc system, or even to reject cruise missiles, is to 'abjure the means of our defence'[21], for a demilitarised Europe would be at the mercy of its all-powerful Eastern neighbour. Thus Conor Cruise O'Brien criticises END, not only for what he thinks will be its differential impact (a point which I take up later), but also because in his view its very *objective* favours the Soviet Union:

> The END campaign must have a far greater impact in Western Europe... It has an inherent momentum towards unilateral disarmament of Western Europe, leaving Soviet power and armament intact... Such a Western Europe would be likely to be incorporated, in one way or another, over a period of years, into the Soviet system.[22]

Now as E.P. Thompson wrote in reply to Dr O'Brien, such an argument cannot be refuted, inasmuch as it relies on 'futurology', on an assessment of Soviet intentions which *might* prove correct. This assessment informs NATO thinking throughout: it is assumed that the USSR would, if not prevented by a nuclear-armed NATO, seek to incorporate the whole of Europe into its 'Empire'. This view of the 'Soviet threat' is held by most establishment politicians and by many ordinary people in the NATO countries. It is also held by some Eastern European dissidents,[23] whose testimony might seem especially weighty, for their experience of oppression, harrassment and military invasion can be invoked as empirical, historical verification of the dominant Western view.

And yet it is just here — in the inference that because the USSR has acted aggressively and oppressively around its borders (Eastern Europe, Afghanistan), it therefore has *expansionist* designs — that the NATO argument is on its weakest ground. Aggression and oppressiveness can be explained in other terms (which are reviewed below), and we must ask whether the historical record really supports the idea, or 'worst-case hypothesis', that the Soviet Union would wish to add France, or Holland, or Britain to the satellite countries which are already so hard to keep in line.

We must ask, too, whether NATO strategy, which amounts in effect to a promise/threat to blow up Europe if ever the East-West line is crossed, is in any case the most rational response to the assumed threat. Could not alternative means be developed, which would continue to deter attack (by making the prospect as unattractive as possible) without carrying the disadvantage that if the deterrent failed there would then be nothing left to defend?[24]

Finally — and this has important implications for the possible *effects* of END — we must ask how far the imputed/ actual aggressiveness of the Soviet Union, and its undoubted and at times bloody repression of Eastern Europe national-democratic movements, has been a *consequence* of the arms race and the militarisation of Europe. NATO may perhaps have inhibited this or that hypothetical Soviet aggression, but we know that it has not prevented the invasion of Hungary and of Czechoslovakia: on the contrary, the 'stability' of the nuclear blocs has been the *framework* within which Eastern Europe has been kept in subjection. We shall see that an explanation (*not* a justification) for Soviet policy since 1945 can be found in what would be a not unreasonable fear of encirclement, a not altogether irrational 'paranoia' which can hardly have been lessened by the decision to deploy, upon European soil, American-owned and -operated nuclear rockets capable of reaching deep into Russian territory.

Which brings us to the Soviet view of Europe. If we make the effort recommended by Bruce Kent, to 'understand the fears of the "enemy" ',[25] we must concede that Soviet apprehensions about Western capabilities and intentions have some considerable grounding. In Moscow, the European NATO partners must appear as accomplices in a military encirclement which has placed the nuclear missiles of the rival superpower all around the periphery of Russia — while Soviet missile bases are confined, or almost confined, to the USSR. The single attempt made to deploy them close to the American homeland led to the Cuba crisis. This, in Soviet eyes, must be the meaning of the European geographical asymmetry. Given talk about 'theatre war' in which an unscathed USA would inflict catastrophic damage on western Russia, given eager efforts at recruitment (or re-recruitment) of new NATO members (Greece, Spain), given in particular the growing, and utterly irresponsible, military flirtation between USA and China... given all this, it is hardly surprising that the Soviet military retains a secure position, if not in the hearts, at least in the public pageants of the Russian people. 'We need only remind ourselves,' writes William Rodgers, 'of those military May Day parades we see on television.'[26] Yes indeed; but then perhaps we 'need only' ask ourselves whether any military establishment could justify itself so readily, or flaunt its annihilating might so swaggeringly, if it did not rely on the threat presented by another military establishment elsewhere in the world. The 'imperialist threat', certainly, is no mere fiction.

And if geography can be variously interpreted, so too can history, and in particular the history of Russia's relations with European arms. Moscow was burned by Napoleon's troops. The capitalist powers of Western Europe supported counter-revolution in the formative years of the USSR (and so played their part in the reinstatement of autocratic statism). The Nazi invasion, which again drove deep into the territory of Russia, cost twenty million Soviet lives. These must be salient facts in any Soviet view of history, which can scarcely begin in 1945; and the brutal coercion which, since the end of World War II, has maintained the Soviet grip upon its European satellites can well be seen as evidence, not of any desire to mount a westward invasion, but of a determination to hinder invasion *from* the west by establishing a buffer zone of 'loyal' nations. Soviet invocations of 'socialist solidarity' meet with justifiable scepticism in much of Eastern Europe, for they are plainly ideological justifications for a policy designed to serve Russian national interests; but those interests (to amplify a point made above) are by no means necessarily dependent upon policies of aggressive expansionism.

If this has been a critical review of US and NATO strategy, and a relatively sympathetic account of the Soviet perspective, that is because I am writing for western readers, and countering a pervasive bias. I have outlined this putative 'Soviet view' first of all to remind readers that it exists, and then to suggest that it provides the context for END. I may be wrong about Soviet expansionism (just as, later, I may underestimate the determination of the USA to cling on to her European nuclear bases, come what may, by whatever means are necessary) — but then I have already accepted the reliance of my argument on an assessment of what can only be hypothetical intentions. And the rest of this chapter deals still more frankly in 'futurology', for 'if there is to be a future, then we must begin to make it happen now'.[27] If we let things drift, if we extrapolate from today's terror-ridden 'peace', if we project the forces of nuclear militarism interminably forward, what indeed can we foresee but 'a miserable slide towards a horrific ending'? I understand the fears of those who dare not tamper with a nuclear edifice which they liken to an unexploded bomb;[28] but what if it is a time-bomb, which is *certain* to explode if we let it go ticking on?

We cannot be paralysed by our own fear. We have to decide what we *want*, and how we are going to try for it. It is my own view that a European nuclear-free zone, far from being a 'non-starter' as a 'step towards disarmament',[29] would be a most hopeful advance, and that the peoples of Europe have the energy, the determination and the political resources to build such a zone.

Prospects for END: Eastern Europe and the Soviet Union

I have already touched on the double ambiguity which END will have to resolve as the movement's strategy develops. Is the proposed nuclear-free zone to cover only the political territory of Europe, or is it to include the western USSR? And how is the political aspect of END, its commitment to the cause of open East-West dialogue and of human rights, to be integrated with the explicit primary goal of nuclear disarmament? Both questions will be discussed by END activists, but the answers must finally depend on the response which END, to date an overwhelmingly Western movement, can elicit in the East.

So far as the geographical definition is concerned, it is my view that the wider zone, 'from the Urals to the Atlantic ocean', which I regard as the desirable ultimate objective, would in any case be acceptable to the Soviet leadership. Empirical evidence supports that assessment: previous suggestions for a nuclear-free Europe have originated in the East or in Scandinavia;[30] the Soviet Union has advanced a great many disarmament proposals, several of which have had a European focus;[31] and that the Soviets are at any rate ready to negotiate has been clear both from the run-up to the cruise missile decision, when 20,000 Russian troops and 1,000 tanks were withdrawn from East Germany, and from Brezhnev's repeated proposals for a moratorium on theatre weapons. I am aware that 'peace proposals' are not the firmest indication of an intention to disarm, and that the Soviet Union could, without risking its security, unilaterally halt deployment of the SS-20 tomorrow; nor do I expect either side to behave with generous reasonableness in bilateral negotiations. Still, the fact is that the present set-up leaves American nuclear bases far closer to Moscow than Russian bases are to New York; and a nuclear-free Europe would help redress that imbalance. Therefore it seems probable that a Soviet government confronted by a strong popular nuclear disarmament movement in Western Europe would seek to 'exploit' that movement — especially if it were under pressure to do so from an answering movement of opinion in the East — by a diplomatic initiative aimed, precisely, at negotiating a European nuclear-free zone. To solicit signatures for the END Appeal on the streets of Moscow would, says Zhores Medvedev, be 'quite safe, and not considered provocative'.[32] Robert Havemann, writing from East Germany, and as a dissident, expresses the view that 'the USSR is willing to take any possible step, even a step of great significance, which might lead to the end of tension in Europe, to the end of the arms race and to actual disarmament'.[33]

'A step of great significance': in a military sense, this might well include a withdrawal of missile launchers and bases from western Russia. It might also include — what Western negotiators in bilateral or multilateral talks would certainly press for — agreements on conventional force levels. What, though, of the political objectives of END — greater autonomy of Eastern European nations, greater freedom of expression and organisation within them, more open discourse between East and West? Surely a movement pressing the USSR in those directions can expect, not concessions, but a frank rebuff?

The first point to make here is that the political goal of END will be pressed for explicitly only in a limited sense, insofar as political questions are pertinent to the building of an authentic Eastern European peace movement (this point is amplified below). The wider political objective should be conceived not as a 'demand' which we must make now, but as the probable *effect* of a less militarised Europe. I have been suggesting that military and political factors, the growth of the nuclear arsenals and the assertion of superpower hegemony over client states, are inextricably linked as causes of Europe's malaise. The restoration of European health thus comprises a double cure; and to lighten the pressure of nuclear confrontation may well be a precondition for a lightening of political oppression. This point is made by Andras Hegedus, a signatory of the END Appeal and a former Hungarian Prime Minister, in an interesting article printed in the third *END Bulletin*:

> It is conceivable that, especially if the factors helping the maintenance of peace were to strengthen, the atmosphere of mutual threat which generally subsists between the representatives of great power rule (and which now is one of the most important animators not only of military preparations, *but also of attempts at hegemony*) might gradually be dispersed. [Emphasis added.][34]

In this reciprocally reinforcing process, political liberalisation might then further diminish European tension, as civil liberties in the East — which must undoubtedly be strengthened and sustained in a truly peaceful Europe — were allowed to develop in ways which the hawkish surveillance of the Soviet superpower has hitherto inhibited.

But if the wider political goal of END is largely something we must hope to gain as a consequence of our success as a disarmament movement, this cannot mean that END activists should abandon their present commitment to the defence of 'free exchanges of ideas and between persons' and of 'civil rights of independent-minded persons'.[35] END's very basis, after all, is in a conviction that questions of ethics, of principle, of human suffering cannot be excluded from political discourse because, if they are, nuclear weapons and the suppression of liberties are among the results. There is, moreover, one area where END's political goals can, and should, be explicitly advanced. We can strive to build a peace movement in Eastern Europe which will reflect both our opposition to nuclear weapons and our democratic and libertarian principles.

END, writes E.P. Thompson:

> entails a definite, but limited, commitment to the cause of human rights. It is definite, because it is necessary also to the movement's autonomy, and necessary also to the remaking of Europe. It is limited, in the sense that an autonomous peace movement cannot intervene in the particular cases and occasions of each nation's life (except where these concern the identity and relations of the peace movement itself).[36]

The 'autonomous peace movement' which will make up the 'Eastern half' of END will, in other words, *itself* be a focus, and an expression, of democratic forces within the Warsaw Pact nations; those who promote it will seek the support of all those (whatever their standing vis-a-vis the state) who share its aims; and the defence of the 'human rights' of its supporters will fall within the scope of END's commitment.

This must obviously imply a critical and tentative relationship with the communist establishment — though it need not, and in my view should not, exclude dialogue with official bodies in the East. There is every reason why parliamentarians in Belgium or Britain should be discussing disarmament with their counterparts in Poland or Hungary. Western END activists need not reject out of hand the possibility of contacts with of-

50

ficially sponsored Eastern peace organisations, so long as these are prepared to find some basis for their side of the dialogue other than slavish adherence to Soviet policy and official ideology. Andras Hegedus insists that it is an error to regard the Eastern establishment as uniformly anti-democratic:

> I am not restricting the concept of progressive forces to marginal opposition groups, since such moves [towards the expansion of democracy] are perfectly visible within the power structure itself and in groups associated with it.[37]

In Poland, we know, many Communist Party members have been active in Solidarity, and have also been working, in the 'lateral movement', for a democratisation of the party itself. This contradictory pattern is visible, too, in the relations between the Warsaw Pact allies: while in Prague Presidents Husak and Brezhnev were jointly rattling their sabres at the Polish workers, President Ceausescu was insisting in Bucharest that democratic trade union activity should be fostered in socialist states. Without proposing any identity between East and West, we must acknowledge that there is, *mutatis mutandis*, a similarity, in that the establishment which administers the status quo is also the mechanism through which much dissenting and progressive opinion can in various ways make itself felt. END will undoubtedly have allies — influential allies, what is more — within the communist establishment, and must seek to involve them in the common work. Those allies will not include prime ministers, defence ministers or heads of the security services; they are likely to be found in more obscure positions; but then that is also very largely true of Western parliamentarians.

If it would be mistaken to speak exclusively to dissidents and 'marginal opposition groups', we must of course still seek a dialogue with such people. But here, too, there is a danger of over-simplification, for the fiction of a homogeneous anti-Soviet and pro-Western 'dissident movement' has been assiduously promoted by the Western media — who devoted few headlines to the signing of the END Appeal by the distinguished 'internal' and external emigrés, Roy and Zhores Medvedev. Again the reality is more complex, for the support for END of Robert Havemann and the Medvedev brothers witnesses to their conviction that NATO's nuclear armoury cannot advance the cause of liberty in the East.

There are of course dissidents who take a different view, the view argued in an open letter to E.P. Thompson by 'Vaćlav Racek' (the pseudonym of a Czechoslovak oppositionist). According to Racek, END, if it proceeds along the lines and according to the assumptions with which it has started out, must succour Soviet imperialism; it 'becomes... a very influential force which works unconsciously in the interests of a totalitarian system whose aim is world domination based on the liquidation of human rights.'[38]

This position is (give or take that 'unconsciously') very close to that of NATO propagandists in the West. Thompson's closely-argued rejection of the charge, which will already be familiar to some readers, reviews at length the question of END's relations with such dissidents, whose courage, tenacity and democratic commitment demand that Western peace activists strive to maintain and extend discussion with them. Nevertheless Racek's arguments, and the form in which they are put, compel what is certainly a difficult recognition — namely the recognition that some Eastern oppositionists, whose dissent is suppressed by administrative and police terror which we must in any case unreservedly condemn, base their view of the world on premises which progressive Western opinion cannot share. To assume that official communist news agencies always invert the truth, and that The Voice of America reveals it, is to end up endorsing (for instance) the murder of Allende and the dictatorship of Pinochet.[39] We cannot make common cause with people who see the world like that. The terms of a potential alliance with Eastern dissidents are the same as the terms of any other alliance, with official or unofficial groups or persons, East or West. In the autonomous European peace movement, 'anti-Soviet' cannot imply 'pro-American' — any more than 'anti-American' can imply 'pro-Soviet'. If we speak to one another in that language, we are simply parroting the terminology of our oppressors, the Cold War dichotomy of either-or. The discourse we need begins in another place, not just metaphorically, but literally. It begins in the territory of Europe: not a Europe dominated by the superpowers, but a Europe which does not exist and which we are determined to create.

It is within this framework, or something like it, that I believe END is most likely to evolve in the East. The question remains as to what kind of Eastern European movement, concretely, is likely to emerge in the coming months and years. Since this *is* a concrete question, it depends crucially on the exertions of people, on the energy (and the numbers) of activists in END's 'lateral committees' — trade unionists, churchgoers, parliamentarians, and others.

These people are going to make their influence felt. We need not expect, soon or ever, to see CND-style marches: too much has been made (for instance by Conor Cruise O'Brien)[40] of Roy Medvedev's insistence that such manifestations will not be possible in the USSR. This is anything but surprising, when we all know that public demonstrations of dissent have never been part of Soviet political life. More serious for END is Medvedev's pessimistic assessment of the possibilities for any kind of opposition:

> Opposition can be expressed by a few individuals, but their influence is not large... I consider it to be unrealistic, at the present time, to expect that official Soviet policy will be changed as a result of open public debate and pressure from below.[41]

We must note, however (as Dr O'Brien conspicuously did not), the context of these remarks: the failure of the Western peace movement even to enforce ratification of SALT II, let alone to influence American foreign policy and to inhibit its growing anti-Sovietism (Medvedev is especially insistent on the folly of the USA-Chinese military rapprochement). If an effective Western challenge is mounted to NATO and US strategies, Russian popular sentiment, says Medvedev, will begin to examine the nuclear policies of the USSR more critically.

It is in Eastern Europe, rather than in the USSR, that END is likely to make some more immediate advances. We need expect no big marches here either, but it will be a very important gain if pressure for nuclear disarmament can be integrated with already existing pressures for civil liberties and national autonomy. A groundswell of opinion — among intellectual groups, in local Communist Party cells — may in time make its influence felt among more prominent and power-ful circles. Soviet diplomacy, which has always spoken the language of peace and disarmament, may find itself encouraged to take those terms seriously. Eastern European nations, if they can begin to emancipate themselves from superpower bureau-cratic control, may take steps, not towards the 'freedom' of-fered by NATO or the IMF (such steps would be fatally dangerous, it is clear), but towards a goal shared by nations in the West — the goal of a truly freer, and nuclear-free, Europe.

These are perilous and depressing days. We are going to need time — years — for the building of our movement; and there are moments when one doubts if we are going to be given time, for that or for anything. All too possible 'worst cases' lie in wait for us. The Americans seem so bent on ordering their 'allies' around that one wonders if political resistance will suf-fice to inhibit their plans — but we shall have to mount that resistance, anyway. In the East, every step towards democracy and autonomy brings threatening 'communiqués' from Moscow. Perhaps Poland will be 'intervened' in — many Western rightists would love that, and their menacing strategies are surely encouraging the Soviet hard-liners. If that 'intervention' comes, it is imperative that END activists take it, not as the final blow to their hopes, but as the bitterest confirmation of their political analysis, and as the most tragic evidence yet that NATO's nuclear armoury, *especially* with its latest 'generation' of mass-murdering missiles, can and will do nothing to advance the cause of human rights. E.P. Thompson warned 'Václav Racek' to look for no help from the likes of Alexander Haig or Winston Churchill: 'the only help which they will bring you will be terminal: a European theatre war.'[42]

Prospects for END: the NATO bloc

The Brussels demonstration of Easter 1981 served notice on NATO HQ that in Western Europe END could already mobilise a large, diverse and international backing. It will not be easy to build up an integrated organisation from movements whose members and representatives (unlike their military-bureaucratic adversaries) will not be ferried by jet at government expense from capital to capital. But the organisational problems will be solved, and political disagreement will be regulated within the movement, since everyone is determined to mount a unified and co-ordinated campaign.

How large, then, can this campaign become? In what ways, and to what effect, will it exert its influence? What will be the American diplomatic and military response — and what will be the response of the American people?

In the two chapters which follow, I discuss these questions in detail with reference to Britain. Meanwhile, abstracting from national differences, we can outline the political context within which END has generally to work in Western Europe. This outline is broadly similar in Scandinavia (where, indeed, governments are less pro-nuclear, and have been quite deaf to calls for 'modernisation'), Holland, Belgium, West Germany and Britain. The cases of France and Italy are rather different. France plays an anomalous role inside/outside NATO, and possesses a 'deterrent' much more truly 'independent' than is Britain's. In Italy, the issue of nuclear weapons, and specifically of the cruise missile, does not seem to figure on the political agenda. Since the Italian left has a continuing and major parliamentary presence, we may hope that this will change — especially since Italy now looks like the only host country where the cruise decision can be easily made to stick. Perhaps Italian socialists have not yet realised what the USAF has in store for them?[43]

In Norway and Denmark, Holland and Belgium, West Germany and Britain, opposition to NATO's nuclear plans, and specifically to the stationing of cruise and Pershing II missiles, has been expressed by a spontaneous single-issue mass movement, whose influence has made itself felt, without exception though in varying degrees, within official parliamentary politics. This movement, which END aims to coordinate, brings together all those opposed to the nuclear militarisation of Western Europe, and is supported by feminists, socialists, ecologists, libertarians, religious organisations — and countless individuals. Over the last year it has grown enormously, it continues to grow, and it has already established an international basis which directly confronts the 'internationalism' of NATO.

This is also more than a single-issue campaign: the conditions in which it works compel it to become, more generally, a campaign of democratic resistance. We have to challenge and outflank the military and military-propaganda institutions of our own countries; we have to create an authentic public opinion in place of a sullen media-dieted 'consensus'; we have to recapture our political institutions, and through them exert our democratic control over a military-bureaucratic-diplomatic apparatus that is growing dangerously unaccountable. This was dramatised at Brussels: on the one hand, a mass of activists, obliged to educate, agitate, communicate outside, or on the fringes of, established political life; on the other — and guarded by riot police — the HQ of NATO, *the* key institution of post-war Western Europe, massively funded by all its member states, enjoying ready access to a largely compliant press, radio and television network, and deploying a military arsenal sufficient to extinguish life many times over right across the continent.

In this contest between a popular movement and the organs (national and transnational) of the state, we must expect to find political parties, whose role it is to mediate between those two terms, in an ambiguous position. This is certainly true of the British Labour Party (whose case is examined in chapter 4). In the German Federal Republic, socialist and social democratic politicians — whose government, what is more, is actually presiding over the planned installation of cruise and Pershing II missiles[44] — find themselves caught between increasing anti-nuclear pressure from below (from party activists, from the general public), and the state's historic subservience to NATO. So Chancellor Schmidt has the classic 'problem' of labour and socialist leaders: how, as a BBC correspondent recently put it, is he to 'control his members'?[45] Chancellor Schmidt's predicament, and the undesirable consequences of his losing 'control' over *this* issue, have exercised the minds of NATO foreign ministers, who when they met in Rome in May 1981 succeeded in committing the Reagan administration to the resumption of arms control negotiations.

Twice diluted — first by the Chancellor's 'responsible' leadership, then again by that hardly radical NATO conclave — the West German anti-nuclear movement has nonetheless exercised an influence for reason and against the bellicosity of the new American administration in the arena of international diplomacy. This is already something, and confirms the judgement of Michael Randle that a campaigning popular disarmament movement 'modifies the political context in which leaders take their decisions, and therefore makes the world that degree or two less dangerous'.[46] The objective of disarmament remains to be won, and in the German Federal Republic, which together with Britain is the key client state in NATO nuclear strategy, the struggle will be protracted and intense — as it will be here. END, meanwhile, has to be consolidated in the West, and the forging of links with Eastern Europeans is a task which still awaits us almost in its entirety.

Let us conclude by reminding ourselves that, while the Danish and Norwegian governments never even contemplated playing host to cruise missiles, the people of Belgium and Holland have been able to reverse the original compliance of their NATO representatives, and have shown that parliamentarians can be made responsive to a mass movement. NATO's Nuclear Planning Group henceforth confronts an opposition which ensures that nuclear planning will never again be the purely bureaucratic operation which its practitioners would no doubt prefer. From now on such plans will have to be submitted, as they should be, to public debate and frank political struggle. In Britain, too, a mass movement has been built, and has asserted a powerful presence inside the major opposition party; here too, despite the flagrant violation of parliamentary and national sovereignty which marked our government's initial acquiescence, the question of cruise missiles — and of all nuclear weapons — is from now on a central, and insistently debated, political question.

3. The Case for British Unilateral Nuclear Disarmament

Recent months have seen an enormous increase in the membership and political influence of Britain's Campaign for Nuclear Disarmament — an increase which the government has tried to counter with a tax-funded 'spring offensive' (which has not, if Brighton is a typical example, encompassed such old-fashioned democratic methods as public debate: while local MP Andrew Bowden warns audiences of Young Conservatives about 'left-wing extremists' in CND, not one Tory councillor has been willing to discuss the issues in public — of what use are local 'Home Defence' plans, should we allow cruise missiles to be 'dispersed' into Sussex?).

CND of course campaigns for unilateral British renunciation of nuclear weapons, a stance which has already gained them a level of support which would have seemed inconceivable until very recently. For example, as late as 1980 Lawrence Freedman was able to crown his endorsement of the status quo ('the role of nuclear weapons... is virtually beyond political choice') by citing an opinion poll which indicated that only five per cent of Britons were opposed to a nuclear defence policy.[1] The figure has fluctuated since then, but now includes a quarter of the population; while the new weapons programmes — cruise and Trident — do not enjoy even majority support.[2]

The rejection of the cruise and Trident programmes, which has been the focus, and the most successful element, of CND's campaigning, does not amount to unilateral nuclear disarmament. There has been, moreover, a new initiative to revitalise the sluggish processes of disarmament diplomacy: the World Disarmament Campaign (WDC) has won wide support for its petition aimed at the 1982 UN Special Session on Disarmament. And END, though I would describe its premises and strategy as 'multi-unilateralist', has been endorsed by some people (such as Brigadier Harbottle of the WDC) who are opposed to outright British nuclear disarmament. 'Unilateralists' and 'multilateralists' share a common ultimate aim, and the various disarmament and anti-nuclear groups have been able, so far, to cooperate amicably and effectively.

However, it seems clear that a unilateralist campaign, or one which includes significant and unconditional unilateral elements, has a far more direct purchase on the national political life than any alternative strategies. In the opportunity it presents of awakening public opinion, the World Disarmament Campaign may constitute a real 'threat' to the torpidity of arms control diplomacy, and may afford an occasion for disarmament diplomats to claim a first gram of autonomy from national defence establishments. The WDC's international basis is also important; and we must hope that the Soviet government will allow the various Peace Councils which play a big part in Russian civic life to circulate the petition. For these reasons, and also because factionalism within the peace movement is in principle undesirable, I believe that CND, while retaining full autonomy, should give support to the WDC. I am, however, very pessimistic about the prospects that the WDC petition has of influencing the process of negotiation. If no progress is made at the 1982 Special Session, it is going to be all too easy for each national government to do what they have always done, and put the blame on the intransigence of the 'enemy'. By contrast, an unequivocal demand for unilateral steps places an obligation on a national government which it cannot evade by pointing overseas.

It also places the question unambiguously within what remains the primary arena of political struggle — the arena of national politics, where governments, in the West, remain in principle accountable to peoples. If we have said (as we are saying) 'No' to cruise missiles, and the state fails to respond, then the question of accountability is inescapably posed, and every democratic force in the society can be enlisted in its resolution — which in turn forces the question of nuclear weapons, as nothing else can, into the centre of political life.[3]

Of course these 'tactical' arguments for unilateralism would be invalid if the case for British unilateral nuclear disarmament were not intrinsically defensible, and powerful.

While the slogans 'no cruise, no Trident' rightly remain in the forefront of campaigning, I believe that people mobilised behind them can indeed be won to support this more radical, but also more coherent, case, and to make the demand: 'No nuclear weapons on British soil or in British waters.' It is support of this demand that I advocate in this chapter.

But I must first make two preliminary points, both of which refer once more to the question of unilateralism and multilateralism. First of all I should like to suggest that it is in one sense inappropriate even to describe a British renunciation of nuclear weapons as 'unilateral'. By this I mean that the nuclear confrontation in which Britain is enmeshed is, transparently, *bi*lateral — USA vs USSR — and will remain bilateral when Britain disarms. The USA will have one less nuclear base, but it is absurd to suggest that any important nuclear strategic advantage will thereby have accrued to the USSR. Between the superpowers, the argument for 'mutual and balanced' nuclear disarmament, in a 'multilateral' (actually, bilateral) process, is a powerful one; but it is questionably invoked where client states are concerned. As Betty England puts it: 'the big powers must negotiate, certainly, but the small nuclear powers can just get out'.[4]

The second point is that British unilateral nuclear disarmament is not a once-for-all gesture, a moment of national self-assertion followed by inactivity.[5] It only makes full sense, and can only be properly advocated, if it is seen as integral to a wider and longer-term strategy which seeks to change the shape of NATO, to influence other states within and outside that alliance, to build a nuclear-free Europe, and to strengthen popular disarmament movements everywhere. To divorce 'unilateralism' from 'multilateralism' is to follow the practice of those ideologists of the existing 'arms control' approach who, to dismiss the practical programme which unilateralism might initiate, invoke the utopian mirage of a simultaneous world-wide moment of nuclear renunciation — a mirage which more critical (or less disingenuous) observers long ceased to discern across the desert of SALT and its (non-)successors.

The prospects for 'multilateralism'

Some advocates of 'multilaterism' are, frankly, hypocrites, who feel perfectly at ease with the armoury of 'deterrence' and have no real wish to see it reduced. Thus Lord Chalfont, who appeared on BBC's 'Panorama' as a spokesperson for the multilateral approach, argued in *The Times* a few weeks later that *any* step towards nuclear disarmament was open to objection 'outside the context of general and complete disarmament' — which 'context' he went on to describe as 'a dream... as far from reality today as it has ever been'.[6] Multilateralism, in this version, is a threadbare ideological cover for the real argument for the continuation of the arms race.

This is not to deny that multilateral measures are preferable, in the abstract, to unilateral ones — a case well enough argued by Dr David Owen, in his pamphlet *Negotiate and Survive*[7] (Dr Owen's actions, both during the Callaghan administration, when he was among the Cabinet 'gang of four' who secretly approved the spending of £1000 million on the 'Chevaline' Polaris missile modernisation programme, and subsequently, show that he is at any rate sincerely opposed to unilateralism). The weakness of this argument is, precisely, that it remains abstract. During thirty-five years of multilateral talks, concrete measures of nuclear disarmament have never been achieved. 'The first UN "Decade of Disarmament",' conclude the SIPRI researchers (reviewing the 1970s), 'has ended in total failure.'[8] Alva Myrdal suggests that 'those who have power have no will to disarm... We are still waiting for a first decisive, or even a serious, step to be taken.'[9] And a similar judgement is expressed still more forcibly by William Epstein, discussing 'progress' between 1965 and 1977:

> In the last dozen years we have had fifteen arms control treaties... As a result of these international agreements and treaties not one missile, not one nuclear weapon, not one airplane, not one ship, not one tank, not one rifle has been destroyed by agreement.[10]

Nobody who consults the history of arms control and disarmament negotiations will dissent from these indictments. Certain worthwhile measures have of course been agreed upon, and it is notable that the best instance — the Partial Test Ban Treaty of 1963 — was implemented as a result of political pressure, both from the international community and from the domestic populations of the nuclear weapon states. Meanwhile other agreements, such as the ludicrous sea-bed treaty, are nothing but an insult to the patience of disarmers.[11] Indeed, actual disarmament is rarely even on the agenda. 'Arms control' is the usual subject of negotiation, and within that narrowed scope weapons are 'legitimately' stockpiled at levels of massive overkill, and upcoming programmes, with their constant qualitative escalation, are exempted from 'control' (as cruise missiles and other 'theatre' weapons were exempted by the wording of SALT II). Such measures represent an acknowledgement by the superpowers that they do have a joint, rational interest in 'controlling' the arms race (even if they do not amount to a very convincing effort at such control); they have an undeniable significance in international politics, as indicators of 'détente'; and for these reasons it is desirable that SALT II should be ratified.[12] If, however, we are pressing for *dis*armament, we have to insist that they have done nothing to achieve that goal.

Anyone who wishes to revitalise (or indeed vitalise) these diplomatic rituals needs first to consider why they have so far failed. The short answer is of course Alva Myrdal's: 'those who have power have no will to disarm.' Since military power guarantees economic and political hegemony, the rulers of the superpowers will not willingly assent to any diminution of that power, and from that point of view their signing of 'limitation' treaties is merely a sop thrown to world opinion. But if they will not *willingly* assent, the question becomes: what pressure can we mount to *oblige* them to assent?

The challenge to superpower dominance must be mounted, first of all, by an assertion of sovereignty in client states, and by an increasing solidarity between such states and the non-aligned nations. Canada recently joined the non-nuclear 'bloc'; it is clear that if Britain, and Europe, followed suit, this would begin to give real influence to what has been a relatively powerless lobby. If we in Britain want the superpowers to begin disarming, we cannot rest content with the advice of Mr Rodgers, and get Mrs Thatcher (or Mr Foot) to beg Congress to ratify SALT II. We must enforce upon our government steps of real political import — at the least, a refusal of cruise missiles. This concrete evidence of rebellion among nuclear clients might begin to concentrate the minds of superpower diplomats.

Apart from injecting urgency into negotiations, such steps are also addressed to the peoples of the superpowers — in our case, of the USA. America (in marked contrast to Russia) has never been invaded, has never suffered aerial attack. A 'diminished reality sense' limits public imaginative apprehension of the fate which most certainly awaits Americans should 'deterrence' ever fail.[13] A British, and European, nuclear revolt might sharpen awareness of that fate, and create a much needed scepticism, on a massive scale, about Pentagon nuclear policies. In the USA, with its democratic and libertarian traditions, such scepticism could take political effect; it is here that we see the possibility of a second, and decisive, challenge to superpower strategies — a challenge from below which accepts that while nuclear terrorism may underwrite imperial hegemony, disarmament is necessary for survival.

Meanwhile, negotiations are very much dominated by the superpowers. They are carried out within a military framework, with its criteria of advantage and disadvantage (and its determination always to secure the former and leave the 'enemy' with the latter), its disposition to hypothesise 'worst cases', its endemic suspiciousness.

For a glimpse of what this means, we can turn to Lawrence Freedman's 'inside story' of NATO's cruise missile decision,[14] a decision which has since been represented as an element in an 'arms control' programme, cruise missiles being no more than 'bargaining chips' which NATO intends to deploy only if forced to do so by Soviet recalcitrance over SS-20s. We know already that cruise missiles were on the drawing board before there was any talk of the SS-20, and we have seen the absurdity of *both* weapons systems in the context of the massive overkill already targeted on Europe. More significant in 'arms control' terms is the fact that Brezhnev actually offered to negotiate on European missile levels *before* the NATO decision was made — an offer accompanied by the unilateral withdrawal from East Germany of 20,000 troops and 1,000 tanks. What was the response of the NATO 'arms control' experts?

> By launching his proposals when he did, Brezhnev indicated that he was worried about the new NATO programme and this by itself offered an argument in NATO against abandoning the programme until substantial concessions were obtained from the Soviet Union.[15]

A 'substantial concession', presumably, would be one which conferred a clear military advantage upon NATO, and which the Russians would thus be most unlikely to make. As for the offer, and gesture, which Brezhnev *did* make, these were seen in Brussels as a *threat*, a disruption to the delicate business of 'constructing consensus' in Western Europe (in the face of the 'high moral tone... coming out of' Holland).[16] But the resolve of that High Level Group (cut off as it was from all contact with the populations it was 'representing') held firm. The Russian initiative was rejected in 'a somewhat brusque manner'. Needless to say, NATO then felt it prudent to 'offer a few words of encouragement, emphasising the readiness to engage in serious arms-control talks, but only after the theatre nuclear programme had been approved'.[17] As for the subsequent progress of those 'serious' talks, they have yet to begin; if they do, it will owe everything to the Western European antinuclear movement, and nothing to the professional diplomats of NATO. Nor need we expect those diplomats to get far in talks so long as they are responding to the promptings of 'defence specialists', for according to Freedman those 'specialists' will be reluctant to scrap the cruise programme even in the event of a complete withdrawal of SS-20s:

> Politicians found the SS-20 handy in returning Soviet propaganda... The defence specialists became unhappy with the tendency to present NATO's own moves... as merely a response to Soviet moves... They became anxious lest a serious concession by the Soviet Union on its own SS-20s would put the NATO programme in jeopardy.[18]

They became 'anxious', that is, about the very events which would clearly be desirable from the standpoint of reason, and which another arm of their own bureaucracy has been busily presenting as the objective of the whole 'modernisation' programme. And for all we know — though it must be insisted that the USSR has shown far greater readiness to negotiate than has the USA — other 'defence specialists' in Moscow, who transmit orders to their own 'arms controllers', are getting anxious too, in case a 'serious concession' on cruise missiles 'puts in jeopardy' their cherished SS-20 programme.

Freedman (whom I am quoting as an 'innocently' frank NATO mouthpiece) is however obliged to register other developments, stirrings beyond the walls of the HQ:

> It seemed that NATO unity had held up well to the Soviet campaign [i.e. the offer to negotiate], until doubts began to be heard in Scandinavia, Belgium and Holland, to the extent that in the latter two countries it was feared that the governments could fall if they pushed ahead with plans to base GLCMs [ground-launched cruise missiles] on their soil.[19]

In the 'former' countries, Denmark and Norway, the basing of the missiles (as Freedman does not explain) was never even contemplated, since popular opinion ruled it out from the start. This, of course, is where *we* come in — we, the people of Western Europe, allies perhaps (so I am assured by the *Daily Telegraph*)[20] of 'the Soviet campaign', but who know at any rate that our voices went unheard in Brussels, and who intend to insist, whether we are 'multilateralists' or 'unilateralists', that NATO's Nuclear Planning Group, or any similar group, must, on questions of disarmament and arms control, be now and henceforth disenfranchised. Those questions must become central political questions, dealt with by elected representatives answerable for their actions to popular opinion, since it is the people who will pay the price should today's game of state terrorism and nuclear escalation spill over into the reality we inhabit.

Unilateral British nuclear disarmament: the moral case

'The bureaucratisation of homicide'[21] infects, not only the military planners whose targets, in the nuclear age, are entire populations, but also those politicians and ideologists who speak on their behalf. Genocide becomes a matter of technical calculation and electronic finesse. Defence policy becomes a matter of 'complicated and abstruse' arguments,[22] arguments — it is implied — whose 'abstruseness' leaves no room for the sensibilities of ordinary people. Mr William Rodgers explains, with schoolmasterly patience, that the opponents of cruise missiles are unfortunates who cannot 'come to terms with the harshness of reality', and whose 'instinctive distaste for defence issues' (actually, for nuclear weapons) blinds them to 'the merits of the case'.[23]

The poverty of such conceptions is well stressed by Michael Randle:

> War may conceivably be justified... Nuclear massacre, or preparations for it, cannot be so. This is a moral argument, but it is impossible to talk seriously about an activity that involves killing human beings without confronting the moral issue. Debates about defence which ignore this dimension, or shift it apologetically into the background, may become highly complex and technical, but are bound to remain essentially trivial.[24]

If the moral argument is essential to a proper *intellectual* apprehension of 'the merits of the case', this is because human morality, especially where it touches on questions of murder and slaughter, is no arbitrary construct: it is a form of human reason. The moral sensibility which recoils from the indiscriminate killing of unarmed people is, and always has been, fundamental to the possibility of civilised life. Our hopes of survival depend in part upon the tenacity of that sensibility, its resistance to the *un*reason of nuclear-strategic 'rationale'.

Unless we persist in blocking out this vital dimension, we must accept that our reliance on nuclear weapons places us in a morally intolerable position. The policy which we collectively endorse might culminate — would certainly culminate, in the event of war — in our collectively inflicting upon millions of our fellow creatures a most dreadful death. Some have wished to darken the clarity of this truth by insisting that our nuclear arsenal exists only to *prevent* war. However, this argument cannot cover the case of the weapons now being introduced into Europe, which are unnecessary for deterrence, and in fact undermine its basis. More profoundly, it cannot cover the possibility that deterrence may *fail*. Where would that leave us morally? For my part, I do not believe that NATO commanders will be 'justified' in burning, crushing and irradiating a million families in Warsaw or Kiev simply because their Eastern counterparts have visited that fate upon my family in Brighton.

There is indeed an irreconcilable contradiction between the nuclear means of 'national security' and the precepts of even the most vestigial morality. In a nuclear weapons state like Britain, this has bred distinct kinds of language, between which we seem obliged to choose; and those who accept nuclear 'realism' will tend to find something naive about the protesters. This imputed naivete is made much of by tough realists like Freedman, Chalfont, and Jenkins, who now find themselves contending with 'men of unquestionable sincerity', E.P. Thompsons 'risen to their full literary and moral height'. Sincerity, moral earnestness — these after all are qualities so little in demand, in Whitehall or in Fleet Street, that those who display them must be suspected either of saintly cretinism ('there is many a fool in Christ', writes *The Guardian*'s Peter Jenkins; admittedly he adds that Thompson is 'no fool' — but why then quote the adage?), or else of something more objectionable: sanctimoniousness, hypocrisy ('the high moral tone coming out of Holland irritated its neighbours'). In order to interpret for the public those 'arguments about defence and security which are too complicated and abstruse to be readily understood', one must first learn, apparently, to speak of missiles capable of destroying entire cities in the same tones as one would speak of lawnmowers.[25]

Human morality conforms, on the whole, with the reasonable needs of people; but the reasons of nuclear states — which engender their own 'rational' political discourse — do not conform with the needs of people. This, far from obliging us to forget ordinary feelings and ethics, should confirm us in a simple rejection of nuclear weapons, whose 'naivete' (perfectly conscious that it seems naive) is an act of political defiance, a deliberate repudiation of a 'realism' which must be challenged before it proves fatal to us all. True reason coincides with morality. And our own chances of survival in Britain, which depend in the long term on the general disarmament which we might help to initiate, will scarcely be harmed even in the short term by the repudiation of nuclear arms to which morality impels us.

Unilateral nuclear disarmament and British national security

These, in my view, are the axioms on which a rational British defence policy should be based:

> (1) Everything possible must be done to ensure that this country is never attacked with nuclear (or with chemical and biological) weapons. It must be recognised that such an attack would destroy Britain and that if it occurred it would be impossible to claim that our 'national interests' had been in any sense preserved.

> (2) Any major war will almost certainly 'go nuclear', so Britain must make it a priority to seek and preserve peaceful relations with potential enemies. The point is not how to 'win' or 'survive' World War III, but how to prevent it.

> (3) The security of Britain also depends on the avoidance of a superpower war, for even if Britain were not a target in such a war, it might well lead to the death of most Britons through radiation and climatic effects, and through the collapse and militarisation of the post-war world economy. Thus, British foreign and defence policy must work actively to discourage the superpowers from adopting dangerously bellicose 'postures', and must unite with other nations in pressing for general disarmament.

I must make it clear, before proceeding with the discussion, that by 'defence' I mean strictly the territorial defence of these islands. I do not consider how, as partners in the Rapid Deployment Force, we might 'safeguard' Middle Eastern oil supplies, or defend 'reliable' regimes against popular insurgence. It is of course true that British capitalism, in the aftermath of Empire, has far-flung interests; and even though we no longer deploy our own forces worldwide on anything like the scale of past years, those interests are certainly protected by our military might and by that of our American allies. If Britain were to reshape her defences on the lines suggested below, this would involve an acceptance that our access to the world market, and to raw material supplies, would no longer enjoy such military protection. In some cases, such as the Rio Tinto Zinc uranium mine in Namibia, British capital would stand to lose — and oppressed peoples would stand to gain. But it is anyway clear that war, and the threat of war, can no longer be used with the old recklessness as instruments of policy: the dangers of suicidal conflict enforce caution, and the responses of the increasingly well-informed and internationalist populations of the 'advanced' nations make blatant aggression less and less politically acceptable. Meanwhile, military escalation spirals up within the paralysis of terror, and is likely to go on doing so until domestic resistance grows too strong. In the long term, however, an international order based, not on force, but on cooperation must come — otherwise there will *be* no long term. If we are credibly to press for this necessary demilitarisation of the world order, we must begin by some demilitarisation of ourselves.

Returning, then, to the framework of a truly defensive 'defence' policy, let us look again at our axioms, and at their implications for British unilateral nuclear disarmament.

Axioms (2) and (3) invoke long term considerations, and stress that Britain's security, like that of all small nations, depends on wider global developments which we cannot directly control. All of us, aligned or non-aligned, will suffer miserably if there is another major war. But the 'aligned' nations of the superpower nuclear blocs are not only sure to suffer more, they are also beckoning on the holocaust by their active, and in Britain's case eager, assent to the military escalation and ideological hostility which make it likely. Thus non-alignment (preferably within a non-aligned Europe), active neutrality — this, in any global-historical perspective, is the hopeful choice for Britain. That choice, and that perspective, are of course scarcely ever invoked by our politicians, who wish to restrict debate to the narrower framework of axiom (1), and to justify Britain's entire nuclear defence posture in terms of a reiterated insistence on the retaliatory logic of deterrence. This outdated nationalist framework must be insistently rejected; but insofar as the debate *is* conducted within it, we must also reply in its terms. And even here our arguments are very strong.

Britain's 'independent' deterrent — Polaris, Trident, the V-bomber force — is in one sense a separate question. The claim is made that it provides a 'separate centre of decision'. If, however, we are envisaging a situation in which a potential enemy is deterred solely by the threat of British nuclear retaliation, we must surely agree that such a situation is one in which the international order and all its political constraints have broken down irretrievably, to the point where nuclear war is in any case inevitable.[26] If, moreover, the possession of national nuclear arsenals is accepted as a legitimate requisite of national security, then the way is open for every nation capable of doing so to build up its own stockpile. If *this* is how we are all to render ourselves 'secure', we shall soon end up in a world of uncontrolled proliferation, where the likelihood of nuclear war becomes greater with every passing year, and in which Britain would stand no better chance of long-term survival than any other state. And indeed we are far down the road to such a world, and have not long to retrace our steps.

The essential question, however, concerns all the nuclear weapons deployed (or serviced) in Britain, the great majority of which are, of course, American. The logic of retaliation applies (or does not apply) even if the insignificant, and ruinously expensive,[27] British nuclear forces are removed from the equation. This logic is actually neither 'complex' nor 'abstruse', but merely asserts that so long as we can respond in kind to a Soviet nuclear attack, that attack will never come. 'The only nuclear weapon used in war,' *Times* readers were reminded by Lord Chalfont (who appears to have forgotten that *two* such weapons were 'used'), 'was dropped on a country which had none of its own.'[28] This argument by historical analogy entirely ignores the changed circumstances of today. It is nonetheless undeniable that a situation *might* arise in which an enemy would refrain from attacking us only because we were in a position to retaliate. To that extent the argument is unanswerable; to that extent, a Britain with no nuclear weapons would be more vulnerable than it is today.

The objection to this argument is based on a different, and

much more realistic, estimate of what is actually likely (as opposed to hypothetically possible) in the modern world. We know very well that if a nuclear war does break out, attacks will be directed primarily at countries where nuclear weapons *are* deployed. Who can doubt that in the eyes of Soviet missile commanders Britain, with its dense concentration of bases, is a priority target? And who can doubt, *pace* Lord Chalfont's analogy, that in the event of World War III Hiroshima, this time, would be a good deal safer than Greenham Common — although (or rather, because) Japan's experience in 1945 has not convinced it of the 'deterrent' argument? In this sense the security of Britain, and of Europe, will be much strengthened if the nuclear arsenals of the superpowers come to be deployed strictly on superpower territory. The maps of Europe in the nuclear games-rooms will then no longer be thick with missile bases, communications facilities, warhead stores and other top priority targets.

Let us recall, finally, that we are supposed to be speaking about British national security. If that is what we *are* talking about, let us remember that current policies place our fate squarely in the hands of a foreign power. Decisions made on the far side of the Atlantic, by leaders over whom we do not enjoy even nominal control, could lead to the death of most Britons. The 'single-key' cruise missiles, sited on British territory but under the sole control of the US military, will only be the latest instance of this. Assurances that 'Britain' will be consulted on their use must be taken a little sceptically: for already — in the recent computer-generated alerts, in the farce of the Iranian 'rescue' — USAF nuclear planes based here have been put on the alert without our government being informed, let alone consulted. Moves to deprive our American allies of 'airstrip one' will involve intense political struggle and can only lead, if successful, to a restructuring of NATO — matters which are discussed below. Times will be tense, the struggle will carry its own risks, and it is understandable that some people recoil from any such prospect, arguing that 'our nuclear world needs to be handled with care' and that therefore perhaps we had better carry on as we are.[29] Carrying on as we are means, among other things, accepting that the British people are more than fifty million nuclear hostages, whose fate depends on the

Pentagon — an arrangement which it is difficult to justify in the name of British national security.

British nuclear disarmament, NATO, and the American reaction

For over three decades, the security of Britain has in fact been conceived of, by political leaders, exclusively within the NATO framework. Whether, and how far, NATO assures our security is essentially a European question, which we considered in the last chapter. And British nuclear disarmament is also a European question, for it must in any event profoundly affect the shape of the Alliance, and may well form part of a concerted European initiative.

If such an initiative gathers sufficient momentum (and it is already underway), a nuclear disarmed Britain need not seek at once to leave NATO, for NATO might then become a forum for *dis*armament, and ultimately the agency of its own self-dissolution. This would be a long process, and would depend on reciprocal movements in the East; but the prospect is not altogether utopian. It would allow the United States to retain some control, and would give it an assurance that its cooperation was still valued. If the unilateral moves of Western European nations can be fused together, and can then involve both superpowers in phased multilateral agreements, the risks and tensions of disarmament will be greatly lessened.

However, it is possible that the United States, faced with a British government requesting it to remove its nuclear bases, might resort to a quite different 'diplomacy', which would not accept the decision and try to build upon it (and upon similar decisions in Holland, Belgium and perhaps West Germany) a new European strategy, but would deploy instead the full repertoire of threat and punishment available to it as the world's major capitalist power and the orchestrator of the International Monetary Fund. Indeed it is not so much possible as certain that the threat at least of economic reprisals would be brought to bear. The full story of how American influence, overt and covert, has shaped British foreign policy since 1945 will never be written, since much of the material is classified and likely to be destroyed. But a light is cast here and there —

72

by the passage in Harold Wilson's memoirs where he explains that an incomes policy was the quid pro quo for dollar loans, by the investigations of journalists such as Duncan Campbell of the *New Statesman* (who has shown how many thousands of Britons have their phones directly tapped by the CIA), by research into the funding by American Intelligence and NATO of 'labour' and 'free world' organisations like the Labour and Trade Unions Press Service.[30] Within what has been a largely favourable 'consensus', this process of unresisted bribery, licensed espionage and political manipulation has worked well enough. If the consensus collapsed, and the process began to fail, what new measures might be taken?

It seems unlikely that the USAF would flatly defy British sovereignty and refuse to remove its nuclear weapons. The repercussions at home would make that a difficult course, politically: here at last the 'special relationship' might work in our favour. But there is no reason to think that a US President would feel inhibited from taking some sort of revenge against a Britain which had become, after decades of subservience, a nuclear rebel. Those of us who advocate such rebellion must accept that possible consequence, discuss it openly, and say why we are prepared to pay the price. Unilateral disarmament would represent a significant break with the foreign policy of thirty-five years, it would be an attempt to loosen up the bloc system which has paralysed Europe for so long, and it might well be interpreted as an act of defiance against the world's richest and most heavily-armed power. Disarmament campaigners, and any left politicians in the Parliamentary Labour Party who desire to be taken seriously on the issue, must begin to accept frankly those horizons of the debate. This sense of a fundamental choice in the making, of a resistance mounted at last to the long slide of acquiescence, might win for the cause of unilateral disarmament a large, realistic and committed backing.

The territorial defence of a non-nuclear Britain

There has of late been considerable interest in 'alternative defence'. CND hopes to sponsor a conference on the question in the autumn of 1981. At Bradford University, an Alternative Defence Commission, with representatives from a wide range of political, religious and trade union bodies, is preparing a report to be published in the spring of 1982. Michael Randle, the commission's coordinator, has given a clear and informative outline of the issues in the 'ADIU Report', and I refer interested readers to his article.[31]

The question of alternative defence strategies is of course raised by the prospect of nuclear disarmament. It requires political and indeed military discussion outside the confines of the disarmament movement. While it is right that CND should promote such discussion, it need not formulate its own policy (some of its members are after all pacifists). What disarmament activists can do is to insist that there *are* alternatives, and that a number of European countries, including at least two (Sweden and Switzerland) with the capacity to make nuclear weapons, have concluded that their security is best preserved by a non-aligned foreign policy combined with defensive measures designed to deter attack, not by the threat of a suicidal nuclear strike, but by confronting potential aggressors with a force equipped to harass and destroy. As Mary Kaldor points out, modern weapons are highly efficient for such defensive tasks.[32]

A further and more radical argument for alternative strategies goes beyond purely military themes and suggests that the possibility of 'taking over' any country depends also on the social and political structures that are to be 'taken over'. To the extent that a society is actively democratic, decentralised, made up of autonomous cooperating groups rather than ruled by bureaucratic *diktat* and sullen acquiescence — to that extent it is well equipped to resist the pretensions, not just of foreigners, but of its own administrative apparatus. The abolition of nuclear weapons, the reduction of professional military and para-military forces and their partial or complete replacement by a citizens' militia, would themselves both flow from and facilitate more democratic social structures.

None of this can guarantee that we will avoid being blown up — but then our nuclear deterrent certainly cannot guarantee that. None of it allows us to respond in kind to nuclear blackmail ('surrender or we destroy your country') — but then no nation has ever used nuclear blackmail, and if it was thought politically impossible in Vietnam, is it likely to be employed against Britain? If we attend to the probable rather than to hypothetical worst cases, we can surely argue that this kind of defence policy would make Britain a safer place to live in than it is today. In the short term, it might take us out of the nuclear front-line. In the long term, it would provide a temporary defensive strategy while Britain worked, by resolute and consistent action and argument, to halt and reverse the arms race.

And this, after all, is our fundamental goal. It is worth pointing to other kinds of defence (and the disarray of current official policy enforces the realism of a radical rethinking), but it is idle to pretend that we can 'survive' World War III. World War III must be prevented. Beyond the short-term alternative — 'deterrence' or alternative defence — the long-term choice remains: 'deterrence' (and its growing instability, its certain eventual failure), or disarmament.

Britain disarmed from below

I have been considering the question of British unilateral nuclear disarmament largely in terms of governments and states and the relations between them. In conclusion, I want to emphasise that if such a policy were actually adopted by a British government, this would be the effect of a vitally significant assertion of popular and democratic power. In place of the mechanism by which decisions taken at the top have been fed back down for us to endorse, we would have seen an accountable executive made responsive to pressure from below — the pressure of a public opinion which on nuclear matters is already both more concerned and better informed than the practice of 'consensus politics' requires.

This reversal of the flow of power would have to operate at several levels. First, the Parliamentary Labour Party would have to be 'subverted' more effectively than it has yet been (for I concur with E.P. Thompson's view that ' "all-party consensus", and *especially* the submission of the PLP to the "consensus", is the lynch-pin of the whole operation':[33] here the first breakthrough must be made). Then, a government committed to nuclear disarmament, and prevented by popular pressure from ratting on that commitment, would have to take on its own military and civil service chiefs. Finally, Britain would have to assert its independence of the USA, and show that it was resolved to accept the consequences which might flow from that assertion.

Such 'government policy' could only be carried through if the government in question continually appealed to, and thus reinforced, the mass movement which had imposed it in the first place. The prospective struggle, and the context in which it will be waged, is discussed in detail in the next chapter. If it is successful, then 'the British people' (as Betty England puts it), 'for the first time in their history, will decide the country's defence policy.'[34]

That policy will be explicitly internationalist. It will not confine itself to British interests, but will declare that the security of people everywhere today depends on nuclear disarmament. A British government which took that message to its allies, to its 'enemies', and to the non-aligned countries which are already acting on its truth, would not be addressing governments alone. It would be speaking for its people, and therefore to the peoples of every nation — speaking, in that sense, over the heads of governments, assuring peoples that disarmament was possible, and encouraging them to intensify their own efforts towards that goal.

4. Nuclear Weapons and Democracy in Britain

This chapter addresses itself to two questions. The first concerns the past: What has been the basis of the 'consensus' by which the public has assented to Britain's nuclear defence strategy? The second, which is posed by the growth of the disarmament movement and the partial collapse of that consensus, asks whether, and how far, the debate can be carried into parliamentary institutions, and (more generally) how resurgent public concern can enforce itself upon a political establishment which still seems largely bent on ignoring it.

There can be no doubt that the consensus *has* collapsed. Opinion polls represent a debased conception of democracy: the soliciting, from passers-by in the street, of instant 'opinion' pushes to absurdity the tendency of our culture to expect or require political decisions to be made in the absence of proper information and discussion. Nonetheless, it is worth citing poll results,[1] which indicate that while a majority remains opposed to total nuclear disarmament by Britain, a majority is also opposed to the purchase of the Trident missile submarine and to the stationing in the UK of cruise missiles. Give or take such fluctuations as the coming months may see, what these figures show beyond argument is that there has been a large and rapid *change* in people's views. This is not a matter just of the direction of opinion; it is also, and perhaps more significantly, a matter of its *mode*. Active dissent has replaced passive acquiescence — and that dissent has certainly not been promoted by the popular press or by the organs of the Establishment. People are thinking for themselves, they are increasingly sceptical about official 'facts' and arguments, they are going to meetings, buying pamphlets, flocking to see *The War Game*. They are taking to the streets. The conditions are there for a vigorous mass movement: a growing body of committed activists who enjoy growing support among the population at large. And indeed the mass movement has been born: an estimated 250,000 people are involved in local disarmament groups.

I shall deal later with that movement's prospects, the alliances it must build, its likely relations with the institutions of our democracy. In particular, I consider at some length the record, and the current state, of what might seem the 'natural' channel for anti-nuclear weapons pressure — the Labour Party. But if we can speak today of a mass movement, the terms were different yesterday, and might possibly be so again tomorrow. Yesterday, there was apathy; there was collective amnesia. Reinforced by official secrecy and silence, that amnesia, and the 'Doomsday consensus'[2] which it permitted, made up the background of state policy. It is worth examining that consensus, its psychological basis, its promulgation by the communications media, the reluctance of politicians to disturb it with any little shocks of information or debate. Disarmers cannot wish away the reality of popular support for nuclear policies, or dispense with the task of changing people's minds; but we can argue that a 'consensus' of this type, based on and maintained by *silence*, is the one means by which a supposedly democratic political system has been able to repress the plain truth that a nuclear 'defence' strategy entails the final negation of democracy.

We have already discussed (in chapter 1) the horizontal cleavage which in nuclear weapon states deprives the people of effective control over their 'own', increasingly autonomous, military establishment; we have examined some concrete instances of that divide. We shall shortly see how the military, as well as operating a system of weapons beyond our technical control, have found political confederates through whom they have distorted and subverted democratic process in Britain, and have evaded the control of popularly accountable institutions.

There is nothing contingent about this, for nuclear weapons systems are by their nature incompatible with democratic decision-making. It would seem a minimum definition of a democratic society, first, that matters of national life and death should be subject to collective decision, and then also that where a minority dissents it should have the right to take a different course (surrender, perhaps, rather than annihilation). Liberty, in Mill's classic definition, encompasses the rights of every individual dissenter. Such rights, such ideals of collective decision — a nuclear defence policy can have no truck with them. What are we to make of these two propositions?

1. Britain is a democracy.
2. The British people might, at any time, find themselves the target of an annihilating attack as a result of decisions over which at the crucial moment they would have no control.

We know at least that proposition (2) *is the case*. Who will deny that its truth involves a radical limitation, if not an outright negation, of proposition (1)?

This or that national government will of course explain that the nuclear 'decision' can be made by an external enemy; that it is in response to that threat that we must be ready to reply, at ten minutes' notice; that modern nuclear weapons do, in short, make utter nonsense of democratic principles, but that while others are prepared to use them, so must we be. We must ask, in qualification of this argument, whether it is not above all our own willingness to deploy nuclear weapons that makes us the target for those of others; we must also ask how far the argument can cover the case of a country such as Britain which has endorsed a policy of possible nuclear *first* use. More profoundly, we must challenge the argument by adopting an internationalist perspective. The nuclear elite which threatens us is in turn 'justified' by 'our' nuclear elite — which threatens the *people* of the Warsaw Pact. The establishments of genocide reinforce one another at every downward twist of the arms spiral, and between them threaten the extinction of every right, since all rights depend on mere life.

As Western Europeans, we cannot disarm the 'communist' nuclear military. But we may be able to disarm our own, in the reasoned hope that our victory would engender a better chance for allied movements throughout the world.

If a policy of unilateral nuclear disarmament is indeed adopted by a British government, that will be a victory for democracy, not only in its potential international consequences, but also within British politics, where the overwhelmingly important question of nuclear weapons has for years been swathed in consensual silence.

The nuclear weapons consensus

Since 1945, British public opinion has endorsed the identical nuclear weapons policy of successive governments. We have been prepared to maintain an 'independent deterrent', and to accept the stationing in Britain of American nuclear arms — a preparedness which has brought us through Polaris and Chevaline to Trident, through USAF bomber bases to the proposed deployment of cruise missiles.

And yet the consensus which has endorsed all this has never been a matter of broad reasoned support. On the contrary: only when strong opposition to nuclear weapons has made itself felt has the issue been debated, either in parliament or in the media. Parliament had not discussed nuclear weapons once in the fifteen years up to January 1980.[3] It is only under the impact of CND's recent resurgence that Defence Spokespeople are adopting a 'higher profile', and defending in public the policies they plan to implement; and this defence, the government anti-CND propaganda campaign or 'spring offensive' of 1981, has been for the most part nothing but a contemptible public relations exercise. Reticence and secrecy have been the preferred tactics of the state, which has hoped, by keeping quiet about the relevant decisions, to keep *us* quiet too.

These tactics have been helped by the popular amnesia/ repression which gives a psychological grounding to the consensual silence. Threatened daily by nuclear death, you either struggle to abolish the threat, or you forget it, and most of us have spent fifteen years forgetting. Those days are over. Thousands — perhaps millions — have spent sleepless nights and entire days in the obsessive contemplation of what had been repressed. It is this profound and widespread pyschological 'awakening' which underlies the change in public opinion, and explains why this has been also a change in its mode, from passivity to activity. The rapidity and manner of its dissolution shows how all along the consensus was based upon a silence (on the part of those who knew of, and made, the nuclear decisions) which conditioned, and was conditioned by, our acquiescence. For all its long fixity, the set-up now proves remarkably fluid, for once there is movement at either pole, a reciprocally reinforcing dialectic gets under way: public concern engenders information, information begets wider concern. In a space of two years, 'the Bomb' has become what we now recognise it should always have been: a central question of British politics.

We must note, however, that the 'information' is still largely purveyed by marginal groups — principally, by disarmament campaigners themselves. Nor is this a matter just of facts (though the facts themselves, especially about the effects of nuclear weapons and about NATO's latest strategies, are enough profoundly to affect opinion once they are made avaliable); it is a matter of arguments too, of the ideas which are disseminated and the framework within which the issues are presented. Although there has been enough publicity to awaken consciousness (some of it, especially *Protect and Survive*, incompetent government propaganda), and although the disarmament movement continues to 'make news' and to heighten public awareness, the crucial arguments — against cruise missiles, for British unilateral nuclear disarmament — are very rarely stated by prominent parliamentarians or in the media.

So far as parliament is concerned, the responsibility rests above all with the Labour Party, and we shall see below how Labour politicians have been discharging it. As for the media, readers will be forming their own conclusions on this question, and I shall not pursue it here. It is unrealistic to expect sympathetic coverage from an overwhelmingly Tory press; and unrealistic to expect the BBC to let advocates of unilateralism escape for long from such nature reserves of 'controversy' as 'Panorama' or 'You, the Jury'. The mainstream news and comment programmes will inevitably remain the preserve of professional politicians and of such 'experts' as Lord Chalfont. Things may change a little, however: a coordinated campaign, Journalists Against Nuclear Extermination, now exists among professional communicators, and principled journalists may be able to win slightly better coverage — as perhaps they have already done on the *Daily Mirror*.[4]

Meanwhile disarmament campaigners will continue to do

most of their own communicating — which indeed is as it should be, since it is an integral part of our political work to provide opportunities for discussion, and to show that a debate on nuclear weapons need not be something we watch the experts having on the telly, but can take place in any village hall, community centre, youth club or union branch.

Parliament, the state, and nuclear weapons decisions

Implicit, not only in the present chapter but throughout this book, has been a distinction drawn between the people and the state. Leaving aside the general reference, and the theoretical complexities, of the term,[5] it is worth specifying the institutions and agencies which one has in mind when referring to 'the state' in the nuclear weapons context. The list is obvious enough: the Forces and the Ministry of Defence, the military-scientific research establishments at Aldermaston and elsewhere, the UK Atomic Energy Authority, the attendant police and 'internal security' functions. It can be extended to include foreign and transnational agencies — American 'security' and intelligence, the US bases, the NATO bureaucracy — from which, at the moment, the British agencies are obviously neither wholly distinct nor independent.

The defence establishment as a whole has been radically affected by the end of Empire. It has also been (and still is) subject, reluctantly, to economic constraints. But the nuclear weapons apparatus has preserved and enlarged its scope under successive governments. Its activities, veiled in official secrecy, have been little affected by deliberate political interventions such as governments have occasionally attempted in other fields. It constitutes the political-bureaucratic counterpart, in the nuclear weapons field, of the 'military-industrial complex' about which President Eisenhower warned us that its 'unwarranted influence' raised the prospect of the 'disastrous rise of misplaced power'[6]; it is, from one point of view, the means by which that influence and that power have asserted themselves.

Living in a parliamentary democracy, we might assume that our elected representatives had actually made the state's nuclear defence policies — or at least that they had exercised effective control over their evolution, and over the apparatus responsible for implementing them. Between state and people, parliament intervenes — so the belief runs — as the sovereign representative of popular will, and the major means by which the machinations of the state are subjected to that will. However, the history of nuclear defence policy in Britain enforces a rather different conclusion. 'All-party consensus' and front-bench collusion have assured that the political questions about nuclear weapons have hardly ever been raised in the House, and this absence of debate has provided the necessary silence in which effective decisions have been made by Cabinets or fractions of Cabinets. Our authority, nominally vested in the Westminster assembly, has been, so to speak, 'extended', and in an altogether undemocratic fashion, as tiny elites within the elected body have passed power on to other elites within the state apparatus. Parliament as a whole has been excluded from the process — as indeed have potentially recalcitrant Cabinet members.

The procedure is well illustrated by the case of the Chevaline programme, approved (in defiance of party policy) by Callaghan, Healey, Mulley and Owen — of whom only the last-named has to my knowledge offered a (feeble) defence of his role.[7] This affair revealed rather clearly the extent to which democratic control was thought desirable, in these matters, by that — and, no doubt, by the general run of administrations, since Lawrence Freedman describes the setting up of the 'small, private, *ad hoc* group' as 'normal in these matters'. 'Secret and bipartisan policy-making', Freedman further explains, prevents interruptions in weapons programmes, and the 'gang of four' only did the usual thing when they took steps to avoid 'a major public controversy, in which the left-wing opponents as well as the right-wing supporters of the nuclear force would have had their say'.[8]

This, then, is the beginning of 'consensus': in the entirely deliberate suppression of information, the calculated exclusion, at the crucial moments of policy-making, of whoever might want to promote a real debate, or speak on behalf of dissenting elements in that large constituency, the electorate of Britain.

Similar procedures, motivated by the same anti-democratic distaste for 'controversy', were used by the Attlee government when 'Britain' decided to make atomic bombs. Another '*ad hoc* group' was convened, to endorse the recommendations of Lord Portal and divert the necessary resources to the proposed nuclear programme. The official historian, Margaret Gowing, comments that 'although the meeting was being held when Britain was almost at her darkest economic hour with factories closing down for lack of coal, neither the Chancellor of the Exchequer nor the President of the Board of Trade was present'.[9]

A dissenting view, that of Professor P.M.S. Blackett, was put before another, and slightly less secret, committee ('Gen 75'). But Blackett's contribution, despite its author's 'two conversations' with Attlee, was not discussed at any ministerial meeting. Then as now, there was 'much unrest about… foreign policy' among members of the Labour Party; then as now, the problem was of course how to neutralise that 'unrest'. Blackett's paper, certainly, risked raising a whole range of unrestful political questions, since he was proposing 'a complete reappraisal of Britain's foreign and defence policy in the shadow of the almost certain breakdown of the negotiations for international control of atomic energy', and urging that Britain should 'renounce atomic bombs and all weapons of mass destruction, design forces on defensive lines and in effect adopt a policy of neutrality between America and Russia'.[10]

What Professor Blackett could not know, as he twice conversed with the Prime Minister, was that the decision to go ahead with the atomic bomb programme had already been taken, in deepest secrecy, a month before his discussion document was circulated.

The decision by which 'Britain' accepted its quota of cruise missiles (a decision about which the Callaghan administration was also reportedly 'enthusiastic')[11] is thus the culmination of a long process. Here, indeed, the arrangement was made between a British elite and a transnational, NATO elite (and this no doubt is how NATO bureaucrats would always like to operate, bypassing altogether the tedious 'unrest' which parliamentarians still sometimes generate). E.P. Thompson is clearly correct in stating that the episode 'illuminates the degree to which the loss of our national sovereignty has become absolute'. One may however qualify his additional claim that it also shows how 'democratic process has become deformed in ways scarcely conceivable twenty years ago', for democracy has never had much grip on these processes anyway.[12]

The crisis which confronts us now raises questions, not just about cruise missiles and about the whole of our defence policy, but about the health of our political culture. One must doubt whether parliament will ever find the will or the power to assert political control over the nuclear weapons apparatus, when it has seemed so far that the question cannot be seriously raised in the House. There was no serious discussion, certainly, between the front benches in the Defence 'debate' of May 1981. It was a sobering spectacle to see the 'unilateralist' Leader of the Labour Party[13] endorsing an official opposition amendment which made no mention of cruise missiles, or of any nuclear weapons apart from Trident, while he expressed his considerable displeasure with the sole member of the Shadow Cabinet who put his name to the 'unofficial' amendment which expressed party policy as contained in Composite Resolution 45 of the 1980 Conference.

Certainly, CND members cannot — and will not — pin all their hopes on the Labour Party. In my view, however, the Labour Party, despite its past record, is going to offer, over the coming months and years, a most important focus both for the struggle against nuclear 'defence', and for the wider struggle for democratic control over the state.

The Labour Party and nuclear disarmament

I wish now to consider the likely relations over the coming years of the nuclear disarmament movement and the British Labour Party. To do this, however, raises a broader question: What is the relation between nuclear disarmament and socialism? It also raises a related tactical question. Should CND identify itself with, and encourage its members to support, any particular tendency within British politics?

So far as the tactical question is concerned, my answer — for reasons which I argue later in this chapter — is 'No'. The general question is so general, and of such consequence, that I cannot pretend to answer it in a book whose intention is simply to argue the case for nuclear disarmament, and British unilateralism, within the context of existing political and economic structures.

I should say, however, that I accept (as I have already indicated)[14] that peace can only be guaranteed, and disarmament made secure, in a world very different from the world of today. Military power is bound up with other forms of power (which, however, it can no longer, in its nuclear expression, straightforwardly protect); it is bound up with the overall power of the ruling classes in the advanced nations. That power will have, eventually, to be challenged in the most general sense. Meanwhile, what I do claim, and what underlies the argument of this book, is that the threat of nuclear extinction, which is a threat even to capitalism and imperialism, and even — *especially* — to the populations of the imperialist nations and their allies, can and must be confronted in itself. This struggle has to be accorded a specific priority.

This may be where the more general challenge will *begin*. The urgency of resistance, on this issue, is certainly such that it enlists the support of many people and institutions who could not be mustered under the banner of socialism. Socialism, finally, is not a clearly defined objective; we know some of the conditions for its creation, but there is no model to which we can aspire without qualification; its full meaning will have to be defined as it is created. The meaning of any socialism worth our allegiance will encompass an unequivocal rejection of weapons of mass destruction. It will also involve the taking of principled positions on questions where the left has not, historically, an unambiguous record — questions implicitly raised by the existence of nuclear weapons, to do with democratic control over the state and with the relation between humanist morality and political 'realism'.[15]

Returning to the environment of contemporary Britain, we can say that the *effective* adoption by the Labour Party of a unilateralist programme would be a development of great significance. It is, after all, very hard to see how such a programme could be implemented without the election of a government committed to it (though such election is only a necessary, and not a sufficient, condition). In the meantime, in the remaining life (if that is the word) of the Thatcher administration, the disarmament movement would gain enormously if its policies were clearly and unequivocally elaborated by Labour parliamentarians, for the media (in particular, the supposedly neutral BBC), who feel able to ignore the arguments of 'unofficial' movements even when they have attained the dimensions of today's CND, cannot avoid giving a certain amount of space to Her Majesty's Opposition.

Now we know that the Labour Party Conference of 1980 passed a resolution ('Composite 45') which opposed British participation 'in any defence policy based on the use or threatened use of nuclear weapons';[16] and although that policy may not attain the two-thirds majority which would ensure its inclusion in the manifesto, it will certainly not be replaced (as it was in 1960-61) by a reversion to the status quo. Among constituency Labour Party members, and increasingly among trade unionists, it is seen as an integral element in the platform on which the party will fight the next election.

The question raised, since the 1980 conference, by the performance of Labour's parliamentarians is whether the passing of resolutions is to have any effect on its Westminster representatives. The reaction to Composite 45 of William Rodgers, who was at that time Labour's defence spokesperson, placed this question in its correct context — the context of the independence, or self-proclaimed unaccountability, of the PLP. 'A majority of Labour MPs,' announced Mr Rodgers, 'does not believe in unilateral nuclear disarmament... I intend to reflect their position and theirs alone.'[17]

Thus the question of defence policy is connected with the question of democracy and accountability within the Labour Party. Nobody can be unaware of the moves made recently to render Labour MPs more accountable — accountable not just to 'activists' in 'smoke-filled rooms', but to the electorate, to whose judgement party policy (which on this matter the PLP and the Cabinet have regularly flouted) has been submitted. It is significant that William Rodgers and David Owen did not leave the Labour Party when Composite 45 was passed; it was the Wembley Conference, whose outcome represented a crucial defeat for the PLP vis-a-vis the constituency parties and trade unions, which convinced them that they had no guarantee that their views would continue to prevail inside the party, and led them to the admittedly hazardous tactic (career-wise) of attacking it from outside. The Social Democratic Party was clearly formed in an effort to damage the prospects for the election of a Labour government committed to radical policies — including, quite centrally, the policy of unilateral nuclear disarmament. Rodgers and Owen are of course perfectly entitled to oppose that policy. It is scarcely surprising that they do so, for both are involved with the network of 'Atlanticist' organisations by which American and NATO influence has asserted itself within the British labour movement. *The Leveller*, which gives a survey of these organisations and of their revamping in the climate of the new cold war, also reminds readers that William Rodgers was organising secretary of the so-called Campaign for Democratic Socialism which was set up to combat the unilateralist vote of 1960, and whose full-time trade union and constituency workers were paid out of funds whose source has still to be properly accounted for.[18] In the long run it is better for the Labour Party, and for the disarmament movement, that such people should recognise that they are isolated from the views of the membership, and should leave the party.

Meanwhile, NATO apologists aplenty remain within it, and the views of 'a majority of Labour MPs' remain just what they were when William Rodgers left. There is no escaping the conclusion that if the Labour Party is to carry through a policy of unilateral nuclear disarmament, many prominent personalities will have to be demoted, MPs will have to be deselected in some numbers, and a Cabinet will have to be formed of very different temper from the Shadow Cabinet of 1981. By far the most likely prospect of a British government's adopting unilateralist policies, and even of refusing cruise missiles, involves, first, a consolidation and extension of the victories recently won by the left over the PLP. One can, and should, be still more specific: if Tony Benn defeats Denis Healey in the deputy leadership election to be held while this book is at the printer's, that will represent a step forward for CND's policies.

It may seem surprising that the hopes of CND supporters should be identified with this single tendency within parliamentary politics. It is certainly regrettable, in the sense that those supporters, as any activist will confirm, by no means consist exclusively of Labour left-wingers: there are Liberals, some Social Democrats, libertarians and anarchists of the 'non-aligned' left, communists, members of the Socialist Workers' Party, ecologists, feminists, and a great many people — the majority — who have, apart from their CND membership, no active involvement in politics at all.

If we are to account for this seeming paradox — a broad current of feeling forced, so to speak, into a narrow party-political channel — we need to revert to the general considerations which underlie this chapter, and to remember that defence policy is at the heart of any state. Parliament, we have argued, stands between state and people as, nominally, the sovereign representative of the latter; yet in the matter of nuclear weapons parliamentarians have connived at the subversion of this nominal authority. Supposedly the instrument of our control over the state, parliament has been the real instrument of the state's control over us. From this point of view the Labour Party when in office has merely operated as the agent of the state military apparatus, and the struggle within the Labour Party — more accurately, *between* the majority of party members and the PLP — is also a wider democratic struggle, by which the popular will, asserting itself effectively in parliament, would attempt to transform vital elements in the British state.

The threat to the traditions of our democracy is not posed by those who are trying to redefine the role of MPs, and to establish a more effective popular control over them; it is posed by the very real possibility that no effective expression will be allowed, within the established modes of democratic practice, to the views of the determined, and large, minority of Britons who want no more to do with nuclear 'defence', and of the majority who do not wish cruise missiles to be stationed here. If the PLP remains impenetrable to those views, if it tries to prevent the challenge to the state from even being mounted, it will have confirmed the opinion of those who regard parliament as an obstacle to real change, and it will oblige the most active members of CND, who are not going to give up their campaign, to look for other means of achieving their objective.

The way forward for CND

Its mass membership, the public familiarity of its name, its organisational basis and (in my view) the unequivocal unilateralism of its policies, combine to make the Campaign for Nuclear Disarmament the focus for the British nuclear disarmament movement generally. I have already touched on CND's relations with other disarmament groups (in my discussion of unilateralism and multilateralism: see the beginning of chapter 3); I return to the theme at the end of this chapter. Meanwhile, these observations on the future strategies and activities of CND are offered for discussion among disarmament activists generally, whichever of the various anti-nuclear and peace movements they belong to.

The sphere of parliamentary and party politics will be of central importance. It is possible, however, that we shall fail to force our point of view on to the parliamentary agenda, and we must consider what forms of action will be appropriate in that eventuality. In any case, a great deal of work has still to be done in educating, 'converting' and involving the public; and in consolidating the already existing movement, and associating with its policies the broadest possible spectrum of groups and organisations, national and local, political and social, formal and informal.

Returning to party politics, I must first of all repeat that, although I believe that the left of the Labour Party will play a vital role, it does not follow that CND should identify itself with that — or any other — sectional or party-political tendency. Some CND members are of course in the Labour Party (which, realistically, is the only party likely to form a government committed, even on paper, to unilateral nuclear disarmament), and they will obviously be considering the question of nuclear weapons when they are choosing GMC delegates, parliamentary candidates or deputy leaders. But CND as a whole cannot support the left *as such*, or endorse the candidature of any politician on grounds other than her/his support for unilateralist policies.

This is not just because any single-issue campaign has got to respect the diversity of its followers' general political views.

It is also a question of tactics. It is possible that the Labour Party will not form the next government; and certain that if it does, the support of other MPs on disarmament issues will be worth having, especially since there are some Labour right-wingers who will undoubtedly refuse to vote against NATO and US policy. The Scottish and Welsh National Parties are committed to unilateralism, as are some Liberal voters and MPs. As for the SDP, one supposes that its vaunted 'democracy' will lead one day to some form of party conference, at which it is quite possible that an anti-cruise missile motion, proposed from the floor, may be carried.[19] That will be a black day for William Rodgers. Even among Conservatives, I have heard tell of an organisation called 'Blues against Cruise'; and Alan Clark, vice-chairman of the Tory defence committee, has described ground-launched cruise missiles as 'thoroughly unsatisfactory'.[20] If Conservative voters are unlikely to be won in great numbers for the cause of unilateralism, many of them (35%, according to a poll of April 1981)[21] oppose the cruise programme, and that indicates a considerable disaffection with NATO strategy.

What is notable here is that, while in all the national political parties there is considerable scepticism about nuclear defence, and especially about its 'modernisation', in none of them has this been reflected by official spokespeople. We have seen that in the Labour Party a challenge is already being mounted to this kind of 'leadership'. It would revitalise British politics, and further the cause of disarmament, if similar challenges were mounted elsewhere. In the case of the Labour Party, we can (if we wish) support the existing challenge as it develops; in general, we can work with the supporters of all parties to widen, and make manifest, the breach between the grass roots and the leadership, and then to make that leadership accountable to those for whom it speaks. And we will be working to that end by what are in any case the essential means of the campaign: the democratic means of information, education, and argument, centred on the single issue of nuclear weapons.

What happens if, despite our best efforts, the political establishment remains unresponsive, and opposition to nuclear weapons, while extending and consolidating itself among the people, remains confined in the House to a few score of backbenchers? Specifically — for this is going to be the focus — what happens when cruise missiles arrive? There is no way that they can be physically kept out, but their deployment might be resisted by a coordinated extra-parliamentary campaign. This might enlist the support of some of the growing number of 'nuclear-free' local authorities (for instance, in refusing to service and maintain cruise-related facilities); it might involve strike action by trade unionists; and it might comprise the taking, either at the bases or (preferably, in my view) locally throughout Britain, of direct action intended to force a response from the government.

The cooperation of the trade union movement would be critical. Many unions, including several large ones,[22] are now affiliated to CND, and some others, like the GMWU, are opposed to the siting in Britain of cruise missiles. But while the power of organised labour is unquestionably capable of forcing the issue, experience warns us that in modern Britain that power has very rarely been used to directly political ends. Trade union support is valuable, now, at Labour Party conferences, but it is doubtful that it would be translated readily into concrete measures of industrial action. Certainly this will not happen unless many thousands of rank-and-file unionists are personally committed to the struggle, and that commitment can only be created if trade union officers and activists carry the argument for nuclear disarmament into workplaces up and down the country.

As for civil disobedience and non-violent direct action, this has been attempted — by large numbers, over a long period, and without much success[23] — against civil nuclear installations in Scotland, West Germany and Brittany. It was tried without success by elements in the CND of the 1960s. If it is to stand any chance this time, a number of conditions must be fulfilled. It will have to be an agreed strategy bringing together a significant proportion of those active in CND. It will have to be coordinated nationally, with national agreement on dates, tactics, ways of reacting to the police, legal follow-up, support (financial and moral) for those arrested. It will have to involve numbers so large that any sense of risk and isolation is outweighed by a sense of solidarity.

But these are merely the necessary conditions from the point of view of the movement itself. Such a campaign would also, and crucially, have to be 'legitimate', for all its illegality, in public opinion. Its objectives would have to enjoy very wide support, which would have to have been mobilised actively, in a series of events and demonstrations capable of showing that the movement was a massive one, involving a real diversity of individuals and groups, and committed also to the traditional agitational tactics of peaceful manifestation and reasoned argument. Those who insist on the magical virtues of (unspecified) 'direct action' now are at least as naive as those who feel sure that popular opinion is somehow bound to prevail *ipso facto* in Britain.

There is, however, one circumstance in which such an extra-parliamentary campaign would be imperative, and in which it might stand some chance of ultimate success. If a Labour government is elected on an anti-cruise or unilateral disarmament platform, and if the right wing then prevents it from implementing the programme, the time will have come for a direct challenge to the state. I am not confident that such a challenge would succeed, but not to mount it would be an acceptance of defeat. It is certainly vital that the leadership of CND prepares for that contingency (and for the contingency of party political failure in general) and that it promotes debate on it, and on the tactics it would necessitate, throughout the movement.

Meanwhile every local group must recognise that much work is still to be done in contacting the public (lots of people still have no idea what the letters 'CND' stand for), in finding new forums in which to raise the issues, in reactivating passive supporters, in building more effective structures which will involve more activists. This is going to be a long campaign, and we need to develop a strong basis. We must build a social, cultural and political alliance broad enough to resist whatever ideological or other onslaughts are launched against it.

This alliance must go outside the organisations of party politics and of the labour movement. It must win support among apolitical and non-political bodies: pre-school playgroups, YOP trainees, YMCA members, social clubs (speakers from Brighton CND have visited all these). It must work through the theatre, writing, music — especially in the youth culture which has already been the scene of effective anti-racist campaigning, and where lots of bands, locally and nationally, are pleased to help. In the end, of course, it *will* be a political alliance, one which has drawn together a diversity of people, many of them 'non-political', for what may eventually be a confrontation with their 'own' institutions; and it will include elements within those institutions — local authorities, trade union branches and regions, MPs, Cabinet or Shadow Cabinet ministers, councillors, trades councils.

This cannot be a one-sided process. CND groups are going to be invited to bring their banners to anti-racist marches, May Day rallies, demonstrations against unemployment. CND secretaries are going to be asked to speak on party platforms. There is a potential conflict here between CND's rightful insistence that it is a single-issue campaign, and the rightful insistence of other groups that if CND is trying to build an alliance then it must recognise that that alliance is, precisely, the only context in which it can hope to win its aims. Some of the questions are coming up already in connection with the slogan 'Jobs not Bombs' and the argument — not confined to members of the SWP — that unless the campaign against cruise is frankly linked with other demands, it will fail. Insofar as these are questions about specific events and occasions, local groups must resolve them democratically; insofar as they amount to a general question, its answer must depend on the extent to which Britain's economic and social crisis deepens over the coming months, and on what mood of resistance, what new political possibilities, that crisis may engender. Meanwhile, although I believe that mutual cooperation with other progressive groups is desirable, the time has certainly not come for CND activists to think about dissolving away their movement's autonomy in some broader coalition. That coalition might turn out to be only the Labour Party again, unregenerate, and CND's demands might only be forgotten. A disarmament movement which has preserved and enlarged its mass basis, consolidating the astonishing growth since the beginning of 1980; which has evolved flexible and durable local structures; which has begun to root itself in the life of com-

94

munities and institutions — such a movement will play a leading role, and perhaps a key role, in the coming political struggle. If it does so as an autonomous movement, if its many thousands of activists are saying (in effect) 'we take part in a common struggle *because* nuclear disarmament is our *primary* goal', then that goal may be remembered, and attained.

Local activity: Brighton and Sussex

This book has made much reference to 'the disarmament movement', and much use of the pronoun 'we'. These terms have been central to its political argument, where they have been the fragile counterpoise to weightier entities — NATO, cruise missiles, the Ministry of Defence. But if 'the disarmament movement' is indeed an effective factor in today's politics, and is asserting a European presence of unprecedented strength, that in itself is no abstract question, no theoretical construct; it is the concrete result of a great deal of hard work. To describe that work would be to write a different book, a work of contemporary history. If the movement succeeds, the activities of thousands of groups and people will be traced, by the historians of a grateful future, through a welter of minutes, resolutions, correspondence, press reports.

Obviously, the work includes tedious irritations — the phone ringing just as you sit down to dinner, struggles with refractory duplicators in money-starved community centres, leafletting in the rain. Perhaps it is worth saying that it also involves the beginnings of a sense of power, as we mount a challenge which, already, our opponents cannot ignore. It certainly brings the solidarity, the widening of social contacts, the consciousness of a part played in the necessary resistance which, between them, make up a tangible pleasure and some exchange for the hours of work. I mention all this because this book may be read by people who are in sympathy with its arguments, who are members perhaps of CND or some other group, but who have not yet found time to take an active part in the campaign. I am asking those people to get involved.

It is in local activity that the building of the alliance is made concrete. So far, this has been above all a question of uniting the various peace and disarmament groups, and in

Sussex over the last year this has been effectively achieved. A. umbrella group, the Sussex Alliance for Nuclear Disarmament, has brought together several CND branches, a large group (based in Lewes) of the World Disarmament Campaign, campaigners against nuclear energy, and a range of organisations (the Survival Action Movement, Shoreham Action for Nuclear Disarmament, Adur Valley Action for Peace...) more or less loosely associated with CND. The common foci for action have been home defence planning and the possible deployment in Sussex of cruise missiles. Petitions opposing local authority compliance in these aspects of Whitehall policy have been delivered, with successful demonstrations, to county hall in West and East Sussex, and this has led to debate, still in progress, at borough and county level. That debate in turn is involving local politicians, and continuing to raise public consciousness of the issues. Meanwhile, among the disarmament groups, there has not been much tension between unilateralists and multilateralists; and another Sussex-wide demonstration, under the slogans 'No cruise missiles! For a nuclear-free Europe!', will greet delegates to the autumn 1981 Labour Party Conference when they arrive in Brighton.

Similar common programmes have been uniting groups all over Britain; and it is likely that a similar repercussion from the 'first wave' of protest will make itself felt everywhere, as we establish a continuous public presence and as that presence is registered in the institutions of the labour movement and of local politics. The alliance established between the disarmament groups is going to broaden, and we may be on the verge of a new kind of recognition and organised support.

Cruise missiles are going to be the immediate target of our campaign. Almost all disarmament activists are united against these threatening, perilous and useless weapons. Maybe we can keep cruise missiles out; and if we can do that — a first, crucial victory — maybe we can do more. We are building a movement to unite people, not only in Britain but across Western, and then Eastern Europe, against superpower nuclear strategy, and so far its momentum has steadily increased. In the end, perhaps we shall unite with us the populations of the superpowers themselves in the single most imperative struggle of our time:

the struggle to disarm the military establishments by whose agency we now threaten each other with daily annihilation.

We cannot know what we shall see. We may see a steady deadening of our culture under the hand of authoritarian militarism, as NATO tightens its squeeze and continues to legitimate authoritarianism in the East. We may see our houses blown down upon us and our children killed. Or we may see what even those of us who work hardest for it can hardly believe possible: a world free of nuclear weapons and of all weapons of mass destruction, a world turned at last on to the path of peace. Only that hope, certainly, allows us to go on — to go on with the struggle, and to go on living our lives, for a life bounded by the imagined terminus of nuclear death is already no life now. Shelley wrote, in *Prometheus Unbound* (IV, 582ff), of an 'Empire, and Victory' which come, not through violence, but through resistance. Hope and defiance, he knew, must be our psychological resources in what we have all felt, again and again, to be an unequal struggle: we have

> To defy Power, which seems omnipotent;
> To love, and bear; to hope till Hope creates
> From its own wreck the thing it contemplates.

References

Introduction: 'Beyond political choice'?

1. Lawrence Freedman, *Britain and Nuclear Weapons*, London: Macmillan/Royal Institute of International Affairs, 1980, p. 161.
2. In M. Reader and others (eds.), *Atom's Eve*, New York: McGraw Hill, 1980, p. 116.
3. See Elizabeth Sigmund, *Rage Against the Dying*, London: Pluto Press, 1980, and her Bibliography (p. 115).
4. See, for instance, Wayland Young, *Strategy for Survival*, Harmondsworth: Penguin, 1959; and especially John Strachey, *On the Prevention of War*, London: Macmillan, 1962.
5. 'Notes on Exterminism, the last stage of civilisation', *New Left Review* 121, p. 29.
6. See the text of the Appeal for European Nuclear Disarmament, printed in Smith, D. and E.P. Thompson (eds.), *Protest and Survive*, Harmondsworth: Penguin, 1980, p. 226.
7. William Rodgers's bright red pamphlet (written while he was still a member of the Labour Party) is entitled *Defence, Disarmament, Peace: the case of the cruise missile*, and published by the Labour Committee for Transatlantic Understanding, 1980. I refer particularly to pp. 13-14.
8. *The Bulletin of the Atomic Scientists* recently awarded a prize to an essay by Michael Shuman which outlined a strategy by which the non-nuclear weapons states would use the threat of 'going nuclear' to coerce the superpowers into observing Article VI of the Non-Proliferation Treaty. (It should be noted that arms control agreements such as SALT do *not* satisfy the terms of the article, which is about *dis*armament.) Shuman's programme seems a counsel of despair — would the newly nuclear states write off their 'investment' if the superpowers failed to respond, and would there not be a risk of breeding the very proliferation one had intended to prevent? The edited extract from his essay printed by *The Guardian* (15 January 1981) is,

however, a thought-provoking survey of the problems of 'a realistic disarmament regime'.

9. Although it is often claimed that Britain has the world's heaviest concentration of nuclear bases/targets, this unenviable distinction may go instead to the Federal Republic of Germany, which houses the bulk of NATO's European tactical warheads. In the strategists' 'limited' war, phase one would be the devastation of Germany; Britain would be wiped out in phase two.

 A map illustrating the dispersal of nuclear targets and facilities in Britain is available from CND (11 Goodwin Street, London N4).

10. Rodgers, *op. cit.* p. 14 (*heavy type* in the original).

11. See E.P. Thompson, 'Protest and survive', in Smith, D. and Thompson, *op. cit.* pp. 53-57.

1. Nuclear-Weapons and Civilian Populations

1. The defence spending policy of the Conservative government is in a very evident mess: a fresh 'cut' (in other words, a money increase less lavish than had been promised) was announced between the writing of this chapter and the addition of the present footnote. For a full discussion of the decision-making context, and an analysis of the tensions and contradictions which have bedevilled policy, see Dan Smith, *The Defence of the Realm in the 1980s*, London: Croom Helm, 1980.

2. See the opinion poll results for September and October 1980, and for 22 April 1981, published in *The Guardian* of the latter date. The steady opposition to the Trident programme is of course in some contradiction with the opinion expressed by the same samples that Britain should retain a nuclear capability. It is this latter opinion which constitutes the 'consensus', and which has persisted despite opposition both to Trident and to cruise missiles. See chapter 4, below, for a full discussion of these questions.

3. Quoted by E.P. Thompson, 'Protest and Survive', in Smith, D. and Thompson (eds.), *Protest and Survive*, Harmondsworth: Penguin, 1980, p. 18.

4. *Ibid.* pp. 14f.

5. E.M. Forster, *Abinger Harvest*, London: Edward Arnold, 1940, p. 67.

6. This point is conceded, rather too generously in my view, by Raymond Williams (see his article 'The politics of nuclear disarmament' in *New Left Review*, 124). Where Williams is cer-

tainly right is in warning disarmament campaigners not to dismiss the notion of deterrence as self-evidently absurd: for many people, it has represented the means by which the nuclear threat has been *held in check*. We have to convince those people that it will not go on working, even if they are right in their belief that it has done so hitherto.

7. Both the NATO 'doctrine' of possible first use of tactical nuclear weapons, and the concomitant issue of 'limited' war, are discussed, for instance, in Ralph E. Lapp, *Kill and Overkill*, London: Weidenfeld and Nicolson, 1962, pp. 85-87; and in Wayland Young, *Strategy for Survival*, Harmondsworth: Penguin, 1959, pp. 31-38. Lapp (*op. cit.* pp. 104-107) also reviews the discussion about deterrence and 'first-strike' capability as it was conducted in the early 'sixties.

8. And see also his 'Notes on Exterminism' in *New Left Review*, p. 121.

9. For a discussion of the weapons technology and its implications, see especially Michael Pentz, *Towards the Final Abyss*, London: J.D. Bernal Peace Library (available from CND), 1980. The political and strategic issues are dealt with in Ken Coates, *European Nuclear Disarmament*, Nottingham: Russell Press, 1980, and in the essays by E.P. Thompson, Dan Smith and Alva Myrdal in *Protest and Survive*. See also Peter Binns, *Missile Madness*, London: Socialists Unlimited/Socialist Workers' Party, 1980, pp. 5-11.

10. Letter to the author from MoD, dated 7 January 1981.

11. See the *Guardian*, 11 June 1981.

12. See Mary Kaldor, 'Why we need European nuclear disarmament', *ADIU Report*, Arms and Disarmament Information Unit : Sussex University, vol. 3 no. 1, p. 2.

13. The END slogan 'No cruise missiles! No SS-20s!' quite correctly expresses unconditional opposition to both these programmes of 'modernisation'. The SS-20, a mobile missile with three independently targetable warheads, escalates the European arms race. Nonetheless, disarmament campaigners must not lose sight of the fact that cruise missiles are *not* a 'response' to the Soviet programme (which is of course more than adequately countered by existing weaponry), and that NATO planned to deploy them *irrespective* of that programme. This is quite clear from the account of the matter given by Dr Lawrence Freedman, who is by no means antagonistic to NATO: see his *Britain and Nuclear Weapons*, London: Macmillan/Royal Institute of International Affairs, 1980, pp. 112-13.

14. A *New Society* opinion poll of September 1980 indicated that two-thirds of those interviewed felt that civil defence would have little or no effect on their survival chances; and most of them expected to die in the event of nuclear war. Meanwhile Phil Bolsover's pamphlet, *Civil Defence: the cruellest confidence trick*, remains a best selling item of CND literature. Another indication of public anxiety has been the emergence of a nuclear shelter 'industry', complete with its own magazine, *Protect and Survive Monthly*.

15. *Socialist Worker*, 11 October 1980.

16. See Duncan Campbell's article in the *New Statesman* of 10 October 1980. Various pieces by Duncan Campbell, appearing regularly from the autumn of 1980 onwards, have allowed a quite detailed picture of these plans to be built up. There have also been 'leaks' to journalists on *Socialist Worker*, *The Leveller* and elsewhere.

17. William Rodgers MP, at the 1980 Labour Party conference; quoted in Betty England, *British Nuclear Disarmament*, London: CND, 1980, p. 6.

18. Especially by E.P. Thompson (in 'Protest and Survive') and by Phil Bolsover, *op. cit.*

19. These remarks — which only echo what experts from many countries have been saying for many years — were published by the medical scientists gathered at the thirtieth international Pugwash conference, and are reprinted in number 3 of the *END Bulletin*, Nottingham: Russell Press, 1980.

20. Sir Leslie Mavor's remarks were made in a Radio 4 debate with Dan Smith, broadcast on 23 November 1980.

21. Ian McGill's remarks were made at a public meeting in the Whitehawk area of Brighton, early in 1981.

22. Councils get more press coverage if they oppose the opening of a sex-shop or increase parking charges. Never mind, the nuclear-free zones continue to 'proliferate', and the new GLC has declared that it will not participate in Home Defence planning. For a summary of developments to that date, see the April 1981 issue of *Sanity* (the magazine of CND).

23. Quoted in Lapp, *op. cit.* p. 126.

24. This proposal is referred to by Sir Martin Ryle (my uncle), in his pamphlet *Towards the Nuclear Holocaust*, London: Menard Press, 1981, p. 11. He says it 'sends shivers down one's spine'. The question of technical and administrative-political control of nuclear weapons is dealt with (in the US context) by Ralph Lapp, *op. cit.* Chs. 1 and 10.

25. The habits of the 'key-turners' are described in Ian Mather's article on 'The Strangelove HQ' (Cheyenne Mountain), in the compilation *Britain's Bomb* published by *The Observer*, 1980.
26. See *New Statesman*, 31 October 1980, for an account of the planned airlift. This operation is code-named 'silk purse': Europe, it is to be presumed, would be the sow's ear.
27. See *Socialist Worker*, 11 October 1980.
28. The phrase is E.P. Thompson's, from his *Observer* debate with Conor Cruise O'Brien (see the *Britain's Bomb* collection).

2. Nationalism, Internationalism and European Nuclear Disarmament

1. For instance by David Owen, MP: 'the emphasis on large unilateral steps, divorced from the context of any multilateral negotiation... is unrealistic' (David Owen, *Negotiate and Survive*, London: Campaign for Labour Victory (*sic*), 1980, p.30).
2. Dr O'Brien's *Observer* leading articles, together with a reply from E.P. Thompson and a number of other articles relevant to END, are reprinted in the *Observer* pamphlet, *Britain's Bomb* (London, 1980).

    The article by John Cox, 'Goodbye to Détente?', is in *Marxism Today*, September 1980.
3. See the articles cited in note 2 above. Lawrence Freedman, 'A criticism of the European Nuclear Disarmament movement', *ADIU Report*, Sussex University Arms and Disarmament Information Unit, Falmer: October/November 1980, is a defence of the status quo. A cursory and dismissive reference to the possibility of a nuclear-free zone in Europe is on p. 15 of William Rodgers' pamphlet, *Defence, Disarmament, Peace: the case of the cruise missile*, London, Labour (*sic*) Committee for Transatlantic Understanding, 1980.

    Previous suggestions and contributions to the debate are reviewed in Ken Coates, *European Nuclear Disarmament*, Nottingham: Russell Press, 1980.
4. E.P. Thompson, 'Protest and Survive', reprinted in Dan Smith and E.P. Thompson (eds.), *Protest and Survive*, Harmondsworth: Penguin, 1980, p. 57.
5. See the articles by Mary Kaldor and Dan Smith in *Protest and Survive*. See also *The Military Balance 1974-1980*, and *1980-1981*, published by the International Institute for Strategic Studies (IISS), London; Milton Leitenberg, 'NATO and WTO Long Range Theatre Nuclear Forces', 1980: available in mimeo from the Sussex University Arms and Disarmament Information Unit, and in K.E. Birrenbach (ed.), *Arms Control in*

Europe: Problems and Prospects, Laxenburg, 1980.

6. This is the phrase used in the END Appeal (see *Protest and Survive*, p. 224).

7. E.P. Thompson refers to this wider geographical area in 'Protest and Survive' (see *Protest and Survive*, p. 57). A debate as to the respective merits of the two proposed areas is in *END Bulletin* number 5, Nottingham: Russell Press, summer 1981 (see pp. 18-19).

8. The first quotation is from Thompson's article in the *Observer* collection; the second, from his 'Notes on Exterminism, the last stage of civilisation' in *New Left Review*, no. 121, 1980.

9. Freedman, *art. cit.* p. 3.

10. See *Protest and Survive*, p. 225.

11. Freedman, *art. cit.* p. 3 (emphasis in original).

12. The phrase is E.P. Thompson's, in his *Observer* article.

13. See *Protest and Survive*, p. 224.

14. My own view, and the view (so Thompson claims) of most of those with whom he has discussed the matter, is close to that outlined in 'Protest and Survive' and cited in Thompson's debate with 'Václav Racek' (see the *New Statesman*, 24 April 1981, p. 10). Briefly, I regard the social system of the USSR, and the means by which it controls its European satellites, as brutally oppressive, and quite incompatible with socialist ideals; but in terms of international, and nuclear-weapons, strategies, I consider that the West has been the prime author of the arms race and of ideological hostility — though the Soviet Union is now so thoroughly involved in that race and that hostility that-the possibility of making such distinctions begins to disappear, which is why a new form of argument, not based on a 'preference' for either superpower, is more than ever needed. Nonetheless those of us who campaign in the West must insist, when challenged on this question, that the USA, and not the USSR, has been guilty of genocide, has devastated entire cities and forests, and has consequently been the author of the grotesque and still unresolved tragedy of Cambodia.

15. Such dissidents are referred to in Thompson's letter to Racek (*New Statesman*, art. cit.).

16. See the discussions in Ken Coates, *op. cit.*; in chapter 4 of Dan Smith, *The Defence of the Realm in the 1980s*, London: Croom Helm, 1980; in Smith's article which makes up chapter 4 of *Protest and Survive*; and in Mary Kaldor, 'Misreading ourselves and others', *END Bulletin*, no. 3, pp. 10ff.

17. Letter to the author from the Ministry of Defence, 6 February 1981.

18. See, for instance, the discussions indexed under 'Precision guided munitions' and 'Anti-tank guided weapons' in Smith, *Defence of the Realm*.
19. See the books and articles cited in note 16, above.
20. *The Military Balance 1980-1981*, IISS, London, 1981.
21. The phrase is Conor Cruise O'Brien's. See his *Observer* leading article of 6 July 1980, reprinted in *Britain's Bomb*.
22. Article of 31 August 1980, reprinted in *Britain's Bomb*.
23. See my discussion below of the debate between E.P. Thompson and 'Vaćlav Racek', *New Statesman*, 24 April 1981.
24. The question of 'alternative defence' is briefly discussed in chapter 3 below.
25. See *Protest and Survive*, p. 252.
26. Rodgers, *op. cit.* p. 6.
27. The phrase is E.P. Thompson's, from his *Observer* article.
28. Lawrence Freedman (*art. cit.*) uses the image of an unexploded bomb; it is Mary Kaldor, in her reply ('Why we need European Nuclear Disarmament', *ADIU Bulletin*, January/February 1981), who writes of the 'miserable slide'.
29. Rodgers, *op.cit.* p. 15.
30. The history of these diplomatic initiatives is reviewed in Ken Coates, *op. cit.*and in his contribution to *Protest and Survive*.
31. The British-Soviet Friendship Society produces a comprehensive list of such 'peace proposals'. It performs a useful function in this respect, but in general its uncritically pro-Soviet stance puts it a long way from most of today's disarmament activists. I have heard a speaker (Cynthia Roberts) speak for over an hour on 'What Soviet Threat?', from a BSFS platform, without once mentioning Eastern Europe.
32. See Mary Kaldor, 'Why we need European Nuclear Disarmament', p. 3.
33. See Robert Havemann, 'After the thirty minutes war', *END Bulletin*, no. 3, 1980, p. 4.
34. Andras Hegedus, 'The highest value', *END Bulletin*, no. 3, p. 5.
35. END Appeal; see *Protest and Survive*, p. 224.
36. 'Freedom and the bomb' (Thompson's reply to 'Racek'), *New Statesman*, 24 April 1981, p. 11.
37. Hegedus, art. cit. p. 4.
38. *New Statesman*, 24 April 1981, p. 7.
39. Thompson, who makes this point (*ib*, p. 8), does not imply that 'Racek' himself has such a world-view.
40. In his *Observer* article of 10 August 1980.

41. The discussion between Thompson and Medvedev is printed in
END Bulletin, no. 1, 1980, pp. 4-6.
42. My examples — Haig and Churchill — are intended as instances of Thompson's general category of 'hawkish and aggressive Western advisers' ('Freedom and the bomb', p. 12).
43. It is too soon to know what, if any, disarmament strategy will
be developed by the Mitterand government. In Italy, an opposition is now developing to cruise missiles, in which the PCI
(Italian Communist Party) is involved.
44. British readers naturally think first of cruise. We must not
forget that for the Russians it is Pershing II, capable of hitting
targets well inside Russia within *minutes*, that poses the worst
threat.
45. Radio 4, 'From our own Correspondent' (John Smeeton),
5 May 1981.
46. Michael Randle, 'Defence without the bomb', *ADIU Report*,
January/February 1981, p. 4.

3. The Case for British Unilateral Nuclear Disarmament

1. Lawrence Freedman, *Britain and Nuclear Weapons*, London:
Macmillan/Royal Institute of International Affairs, 1980,
p. 161.
2. See *The Guardian*, 22 April 1981, which also prints (on cruise
and Trident) the results of polls of September and November
1980.
3. See Chapter 4 below for a discussion of the relation between
the demand for unilateral nuclear disarmament and the question
(especially in the Labour Party) of the accountability of
representatives.
4. Betty England, *British Nuclear Disarmament*, London: CND,
1980, p. 21.
5. This point is well made by Raymond Williams. See 'The
politics of nuclear disarmament', *New Left Review* 124, which
discusses the whole question of what we mean by
'unilateralism'.
6. *The Times*, 3 December 1980.
7. David Owen, *Negotiate and Survive*, London: Campaign for
Labour Victory, 1980.
8. Annual *Brochure* for 1980, published by the Stockholm International Peace Research Institute (see p. 6).
9. Alva Myrdal, *The Game of Disarmament*, Manchester University
Press, 1977, p. 9. Myrdal's book, together with Elizabeth
Young, *A Farewell to Arms Control?* Harmondsworth:

Penguin, should be consulted by those who wish to look in
more detail at the history of arms control diplomacy.

10. See 'The failure to control the nuclear arms race', in the pro-
ceedings of the Kyoto Pugwash symposium, *A New Design for
Nuclear Disarmament*, Nottingham: Russell Press, 1977, p. 4.

11. On the sea-bed treaty, see Dan Smith, *The Defence of the
Realm in the 1980s*, London: Croom Helm, 1980, p. 217. This
has been compared, Smith explains, to an agreement pro-
hibiting the nuclear powers from bolting their bombers to the
runways.

12. Roy Medvedev emphasises this (see *END Bulletin*, no. 1, p. 6);
so does William Rodgers, who also says that after this 'essential' step, European theatre weapons must be negotiated on in
SALT III. What will he do if these 'essential' steps are not
taken by US diplomacy? Perhaps the Social Democratic Party
will come out against NATO... (See Rodgers, *Defence, Disarmament, Peace: the Case of the Cruise Missile*, London:
Labour Committee for Transatlantic Understanding, 1980,
p. 11.)

13. See E.P. Thompson, 'Protest and Survive', in Dan Smith and
E.P. Thompson, (eds.), *Protest and Survive*, Harmondsworth:
Penguin, 1980, p. 43. On the entire question of the views of
Soviet and American citizens, see Myrdal, *op. cit.* pp. 332ff.

14. See Freedman, *op. cit.*, chapter 11, 'Nuclear politics in
Europe'.

15. *Ib*. p. 122.

16. *Ib*. p. 120.

17. *Ib*. p. 122.

18. *Ib*. pp. 112-13.

19. *Ib*. p. 122.

20. See the *Daily Telegraph*, 16 March 1981, p. 6 ('The Challenge
to Euromissiles'). It is here explained that the mass movement
against cruise missiles is all the work of a few strategically placed
Soviet agents and sympathisers within Western European
socialist and social democratic parties.

21. The phrase is the title of an article by former US Department
of Defense employee Henry T. Nash, reprinted in *Protest and
Survive*.

22. Lord Chalfont, *art. cit.* (see note 6 above).

23. Rodgers, *op. cit.* p. 3.

24. Michael Randle, 'Defence without the bomb', *ADIU Report*,
vol. 3 no. 1, Sussex University Arms and Disarmament Information Unit, 1981, pp. 4-7.

106

25. My quotations are taken from the article I have cited by Lord
Chalfont, from the article by Peter Jenkins in *The Guardian* of
23 July 1980, and from Lawrence Freedman's book (p. 120).
26. This point is well made by Robert Stephens, Foreign Editor of
The Observer, in an article of 27 July 1980; and by Mark
Frankland, the same paper's 'specialist in Soviet affairs', in an
article of 10 August 1980. Both pieces are reprinted in the collection *Britain's Bomb* (London 1980).
27. The question of cost is subsidiary to the question of whether
Trident can do what is claimed for it — prevent nuclear war. If
it cannot, then Trident is a waste of a very great deal of
money: but the focus of disarmers' arguments must be on the
'rationale', and its weakness, not on the cost as such.
28. Lord Chalfont, *art. cit.*
29. This is the view expressed by Lawrence Freedman in his article
'A criticism of the European Nuclear Disarmament movement',
ADIU Report, vol. 2 no. 4.
30. Thompson quotes the passage from Wilson's memoirs in
Writing by Candlelight, London: Merlin Press, 1980, p. 56.
Details of Menwith Hill, the CIA phone-tapping HQ, are in the
New Statesman, 18 July 1980. For a discussion of the CIA,
NATO and the Labour right, see *The Leveller*, 20 March 1981;
and *Militant*, 25 January and 1 February, 1980.
31. 'Defence without the bomb', *ADIU Report*, vol. 3 no. 1.
32. Mary Kaldor, 'Why we need European Nuclear Disarmament',
ADIU Report, vol. 3 no. 1, p. 3. See also Smith, *op. cit.*
pp. 260-63.
33. E.P. Thompson, *Writing by Candlelight*, p. 271.
34. Betty England, *op. cit.* p. 22.

4. Nuclear Weapons and Democracy in Britain

1. See *The Guardian*, 22 April 1981.
2. This is the title of one of E.P. Thompson's most powerful articles on 'the management of opinion' in the nuclear state. See
Writing by Candlelight, London: Merlin Press, 1980, p. 259.
3. See 'Protest and Survive', *Protest and Survive*, Harmondsworth: Penguin, 1980, p. 19.
4. The *Mirror*'s 'shock issue' of 6 November 1980, which had a
dramatic front-page of a mushroom cloud over London and
which was largely devoted to the subject of nuclear weapons,
will have been the first opportunity for many people to ac-
quaint themselves with the destructive power of modern
weapons, and with the dangers of European war. Some continu-

ing coverage since then has included in particular an excellent feature by John Pilger on *The War Game* (March 5, 1981).

5. See on this the discussion in Dan Smith, *The Defence of the Realm in the 1980s*, London: Croom Helm, 1980, pp. 21ff, and his bibliographical references.

6. These well-known remarks of Eisenhower are quoted in Prof M. Ryle, *Towards the Nuclear Holocaust*, London: Menard Press, 1981, p. 16.

7. See David Owen, *Negotiate and Survive*, London: Campaign for Labour Victory, 1980, p. 14.

8. Lawrence Freedman, *Britain and Nuclear Weapons*, London: Macmillan/Royal Institute of International Affairs, 1980, pp. 60, 54.

9. See Margaret Gowing, *Independence and Deterrence*, London: Macmillan, vol. 1, 1974, pp. 182-84.

10. *Ib*. Prof Blackett's paper is reprinted on pp. 194-206.

11. According to Freedman, *op. cit.* p. 125.

12. See *Protest and Survive*, p. 45.

13. By placing inverted commas around 'unilateralist' I do not wish to cast doubt on Michael Foot's personal commitment, but only to question how far that commitment has been evident in his handling of defence matters in the Shadow Cabinet. Of course it is difficult and hazardous to take on the right wing over the issue. But if they cannot be challenged now, who can seriously believe that a future Labour government will keep cruise missiles out, let alone close down USAF bases?

14. In the introduction to this book.

15. For one view of the relations between disarmament and socialism, see *Socialist Review*, 17 October-14 November 1980. Similar opinions are held by supporters of *Militant* — see for instance the article by Rob Sewell on CND in issue no. 584. The matter is discussed from a different perspective by Raymond Williams, who — in my view, rightly — poses the question of what specifically socialist arguments and insights can contribute to the disarmament movement, rather than arguing that the movement starts out from mistaken theoretical and practical positions which must be corrected before there is any hope of success. See Williams, 'The politics of nuclear disarmament', *New Left Review*, no. 124.

16. An extract from the resolution is reprinted in Betty England, *British Nuclear Disarmament*, London: CND, 1980, p. 22.

17. Quoted in *ib*. p. 4.

18. See *The Leveller*, 20 March 1981, p. 10. See also Richard
    Fletcher, *The CIA and the Labour Movement*, Nottingham:
    Spokesman Books, 1977.
19. According to the opinion poll published in *The Guardian* of 22
    April 1981, 54% of those intending to vote Social Democrat or
    Liberal were opposed to the cruise missiles.
20. See *Sanity*, April/May 1980, quoting Mr Clark's letter published
    in *The Guardian* of 16 January 1981.
21. See *The Guardian*, 22 April 1981.
22. Such as NALGO, NUPE and ASTMS. See *Sanity*, June 1981,
    and *Socialist Worker*, 27 June 1981.
23. The new Socialist administration in France has, however, called
    off the planned Plogoff power station, which had been the
    focus of massive protest action over many years.

Pluto books on anti-nuclear and environmental issues

Power Corrupts
The Arguments Against Nuclear Power

Hilary Bacon and John Valentine

The dangers of nuclear reactors of the infamous Three Mile Island type, and the alternative to the Government programme.

ISBN 86104 345 6 paperback

No Nuclear Weapons

Peter Kennard and Ric Sissons

A Joint Publication with CND

A powerful and visual documentary statement using photomontage and text to make the case against nuclear weapons.

ISBN 86104 337 5 paperback

No Nukes
Everyone's Guide to Nuclear Power

Anna Gyorgy and friends

The 'bible' of the American anti-nuclear movement.

ISBN 86104 905 5 paperback

Destruction of Nature in the Soviet Union

Boris Komarov

'A passionate indictment of the Soviet authorities for allowing the country's land, water and wildlife to be despoiled.' *Sunday Times*

ISBN 86104 323 5 paperback

The Politics of Nuclear Power

Dave Elliott with Pat Coyne, Mike George and Roy Lewis

'Sound and sensible.' *The Vole*. 'Lucid and concise.' *The Ecologist*

ISBN 86104 028 7 paperback

Rage Against the Dying
The Campaign Against Chemical and Biological Warfare in Britain

Liz Sigmund

'A compelling history of the development of chemical and biological weapons in this country.' *The Vole*

ISBN 86104 091 0 paperback